S0-EGH-009

TYPE 2 DIABETES

COOKBOOK

365 DAYS OF QUICK & EASY DIABETIC FRIENDLY RECIPES FOR THE NEWLY DIAGNOSED

BY DEBBY HAYES

© Copyright 2021 by – Debby Hayes - All Rights Reserved.

This document is geared towards providing exact and reliable information in regards to the topic and issue covered. The publication is sold with the idea that the publisher is not required to render accounting, officially permitted, or otherwise, qualified services. If advice is necessary, legal or professional, a practiced individual in the profession should be ordered.

- From a Declaration of Principles which was accepted and approved equally by a Committee of the American Bar Association and a Committee of Publishers and Associations.

In no way is it legal to reproduce, duplicate, or transmit any part of this document in either electronic means or in printed format. Recording of this publication is strictly prohibited and any storage of this document is not allowed unless with written permission from the publisher. All rights reserved.

The information provided herein is stated to be truthful and consistent, in that any liability, in terms of inattention or otherwise, by any usage or abuse of any policies, processes, or directions contained within is the solitary and utter responsibility of the recipient reader. Under no circumstances will any legal responsibility or blame be held against the publisher for any reparation, damages, or monetary loss due to the information herein, either directly or indirectly.

All data and information provided in this book is for informational purposes only. Debby Hayes makes no representations as to accuracy, completeness, current, suitability, or validity of any information in this book & will not be liable for any errors, omissions, or delays in this information or any losses, injuries, or damages arising from its display or use. All information is provided on an as-is basis.

Respective authors own all copyrights not held by the publisher.

The information herein is offered for informational purposes solely, and is universal as so. The presentation of the information is without contract or any type of guarantee assurance.

The trademarks that are used are without any consent, and the publication of the trademark is without permission or backing by the trademark owner. All trademarks and brands within this book are for clarifying purposes only and are owned by the owners themselves, not affiliated with this document.

The author is not a licensed practitioner, physician or medical professional and offers no medical treatment, diagnoses, suggestions or counselling. The information presented herein has not been evaluated by the U.S Food & Drug Administration, and it is not intended to diagnose, treat, cure or prevent any disease. Full medical clearance from a licensed physician should be obtained before beginning or modifying any diet, exercise or lifestyle program, and physician should be informed of all nutritional changes. The author claims no responsibility to any person or entity for any liability, loss, damage or death caused or alleged to be caused directly or indirectly as a result of the use, application or interpretation of the information presented herein.

TABLE OF CONTENTS

TYPE 2 DIABETES DIET INTRO

Hundreds of millions of people are living with diabetes, worldwide. Many of these people don't even know they have it. It is often an unpleasant surprise diagnosis when you go to hospital or see your doctor for something else and instead you receive the unwelcome news that you have diabetes.

Almost everyone knows someone who has diabetes. A friend or a family member may have tearfully told you that their doctor has given them some very bad news. Or maybe you've noticed they have suddenly made some drastic lifestyle changes. You may even recently have heard your own doctor say, "You have type 2 diabetes."

It can feel like your world is crashing down around you and your brain is whirling with thoughts. 'After all, people die from diabetes, don't they? And what about my diet? People who have diabetes have to eat special food, don't they? And they have to inject themselves with insulin three times a day, don't they?' Your mind is spinning. The last thing you want is to become a burden to those you love.

It is an overwhelming diagnosis, but let me put your mind at ease. Diabetes is not a death sentence. It can be well, and relatively easily managed through a combination of diet, exercise, and medication. There is no need for special foods. In fact, any dietary changes you have to make are family-friendly. Everyone will benefit from your healthier diet. And as for the injections, most newly diagnosed people with type 2 diabetes only have to swallow a pill or two a day.

As a dietitian, I have worked with people who have had diabetes for more than 20 years. I have witnessed first-hand how terrified and confused people are when they are first diagnosed. But with proper guidance and some tender loving care, most people go on to live a long, healthy life, even when they have type 2 diabetes.

But the threat of serious medical complications is very real. It is heartbreaking to walk into a hospital ward to consult with someone who has lost a leg, or has gone blind, or who has suffered a heart attack, or has to have dialysis to manage kidney failure. All because they have not been managing their blood sugar levels.

You can start taking control of your type 2 diabetes right now. Diet is the cornerstone in the management of this disease. Making healthy food choices can make all the difference to your quality and length of life.

WHAT DOES IT MEAN TO HAVE TYPE 2 DIABETES?

Receiving a diagnosis of type 2 diabetes does not mean that you have been 'bad'. It does not mean that you have brought it on yourself. And it does not mean that you have to be punished or judged.

Other people eat and drink and watch TV the same as you do and they don't have diabetes. It means that they have a different genetic makeup to you. It is possible that you have inherited the genes that are related to the risk of developing diabetes from your mom and dad or your grandparents.

While there is a strong genetic link to type 2 diabetes, having a family history of the disease does not automatically mean that you will develop it too. Lifestyle factors such as diet and exercise are even more important than your DNA. The gene mutations that cause type 2 diabetes can be controlled by what you eat and how much exercise you do. Those with the genetic makeup that are more resilient toward diabetes should also be careful about eating badly and spending most or all their time on the couch. They too, could develop diabetes.

When your doctor says "You have type 2 diabetes", it is usually after a battery of blood tests. Diabetes is characterized by above normal blood sugar levels. This means that both your fasting blood sugar level (when you wake up in the morning) and your postprandial blood sugar level (2 hours after eating) is high..

NORMAL BLOOD SUGAR CONTROL

Everyone has sugar in their blood in the form of glucose. It is what your body uses for energy to power every single cell. Your brain can only use glucose for energy, so it is an essential nutrient.

Glucose is the simplest form of carbohydrate. Almost all starchy foods are a source of glucose. Foods such as bread, potatoes, rice and pasta, as well as refined sugars like the white crystals you spoon into your coffee are digested into their simplest form to provide your body with energy.

When glucose is absorbed into your blood from your digestive tract, your blood sugar levels rise. A normal fasting blood sugar level is roughly 5 mmol per liter. After eating, it is normal for it to rise by about two points to roughly 7 mmol per liter.

In response to the rise in blood sugar, insulin is secreted from the pancreas. The insulin's job is to attach to the insulin receptors that are found on every cell. It then acts as a key, unlocking the cells and allowing the glucose to move in. Once inside the cells, it is used in biochemical processes that generate the energy that keeps us alive. As a result, blood sugar levels drop back to fasting level again.

This is the normal up and down fluctuation of blood glucose levels. Each cycle should take about four hours from start to finish. It all depends on what you eat and how active you are. It could be longer or shorter.

The pattern changes when you have diabetes. Your fasting blood sugar level is probably higher than 5 mmol per liter and your postprandial reading is likely to rise by more than two points.

THE DIFFERENT TYPES OF DIABETES: DIAGNOSIS AND MANAGEMENT

There are three main types of diabetes. Although all three result in high blood sugar levels, the underlying causes are different. All three are diagnosed using the same blood tests:

- **Fasting blood glucose:** A blood test that determines your blood sugar level upon waking, before eating or drinking anything. It is considered to be high if your blood sugar reading is higher than 5,6 mmol per liter.

- **HbA1c:** A blood test that determines your average blood sugar level over the last three months. A reading of over 6,5% means that you have diabetes.

- **Glucose tolerance test:** This test takes place over three hours. Your fasting blood glucose level will be tested and then you will be given a solution of glucose to drink. Your blood sugar levels will be tested every 30 to 60 minutes to see how efficient your body is at removing sugar from the blood. If your blood sugar is higher than 7,8 mmol per liter 2 hours after drinking the solution, you most likely have diabetes.

Gestational diabetes is high blood sugar levels while you are pregnant. This usually resolves once the baby is born and your blood glucose goes back to normal. But you have a higher chance of developing type 2 diabetes later in life. Uncontrolled blood sugar levels during pregnancy usually results in bigger, heavier babies who have an increased risk of being obese and becoming diabetic when they get older.

Treatment usually involves diet and taking oral hypoglycemic agents (pills to lower your blood sugar levels). If it becomes difficult to control blood sugar levels using these interventions, insulin may be necessary.

Type 1 Diabetes used to be called child-onset diabetes because it first appears in young children and teens. The root cause still isn't clear, but it is thought to be the result of an autoimmune condition that affects the pancreas. If you have type 1 diabetes your body is not able to produce the insulin that is required to move the glucose out of your blood and into your cells. Therefore, your blood sugar levels climb uncontrollably.

Because the pancreas is not able to produce insulin, it is essential that you inject yourself with insulin when you have type 1 diabetes. There are different types of insulin that are effective for varying amounts of time. They are short-acting, medium-acting and long-acting insulin. Blood sugar levels are usually controlled using a combination of these.

Type 2 Diabetes is a result of insulin resistance. It is a condition that develops over a long period of time. Your pancreas is still producing insulin, but it cannot be used as efficiently as it used to be. The insulin receptors on the body's cells can no longer bind to the insulin that is released when your blood sugar levels rise. As a result, both sugar and insulin levels rise.

Treatment begins with dietary changes and ingestion of oral hypoglycemic agents (pills to lower your blood sugar levels). Type 2 diabetes is often a progressive disease, so your medication needs to be monitored regularly by your doctor. You may eventually have to start using insulin as well.

CHANGES TO YOUR DIET: FOODS TO LIMIT

Let's get the bad news out of the way first. There are foods that you are encouraged to avoid all together, or at least limit, when you need to control your blood sugar levels. They are foods that everyone should be restricting, not just people with diabetes. They are foods that cause a spike in blood sugar levels, increase inflammation generally, and have an impact on the amount of fat in your blood.

Refined sugar is a definite NO. Try to wean yourself off having sugar in your tea and coffee. This is much easier than just stopping. It allows your taste buds to adjust slowly. Before you know it you won't like tea or coffee with sugar.

Also keep an eye on sugary foods and snacks such as chocolates, sweets, cold drinks, baked goods and desserts. Your body doesn't have to do much work to get the sugar out of these foods, so it is released very quickly into your bloodstream. This causes a rapid and high spike in blood sugar levels.

Remember that all carbohydrate foods are digested into their simplest form— glucose. That does not mean that you have to avoid all starchy foods. But you do need to be wary of the refined ones. The more processing the food has undergone, the less your body has to do to extract the energy from it, the greater your blood sugar spike is going to be. Try to stay away from all foods made with white flours such as white bread, pizza and cookies.

Foods that contain a lot of saturated fat are also problematic. They may not cause a spike in blood glucose levels, but they have been implicated in the development of type 2 diabetes. They also cause inflammation in the body and raise your bad cholesterol levels. Fat on meat, skin on chicken, full cream dairy products, cheese and coconut oil are delicious, but should be limited.

A HEALTHY DIABETES DIET: BALANCE IS THE KEY

A healthy diabetes diet is exactly the same as the healthy diet recommended for the general population. The problem is we tend to deviate from the official dietary guidelines, enjoying too much sugary, fatty foods. Living with type 2 diabetes means that you need to adhere to these recommendations more strictly.

It may seem like you have to make some pretty big changes to your grocery list and your eating habits, but there is a good chance you are going to find it easier than you think. It all begins with a balanced plate.

The goal is to fill half of your plate with vegetables. Aim to eat mostly non-starchy vegetables such as spinach, cabbage, green beans and patty pans. You don't have to avoid the vegetables that contain a few more carbohydrates, but limit the amount of butternut, pumpkin and corn you eat.

Once you have dished up your veggies, add a protein food such as meat, fish, chicken or legumes to fill just a quarter of your plate. Your body's protein requirements are surprisingly small. The ideal portion is the size of the palm of your hand.

Finally add the carbs to your plate. They should take up the remaining quarter. Aim for whole grain, unprocessed carbohydrate foods such as brown rice, barley, and sweet potatoes.

Fat is also important and it is most likely being used in the cooking process. Fats such as olive oil add flavor and nutrition to your meals. Your food definitely doesn't have to be fat-free, but you don't want to go overboard either.

If you follow this simple template on what to dish in any meal, you are more than halfway there.

THE BEST FOODS TO INCLUDE IN YOUR NEW DIET

Now for the good news! There is a long list of foods that are allowed and encouraged in a type 2 diabetes diet. The list below is not extensive, but it is a great place to start.

FOOD GROUP	RECOMMENDED FOODS
MILK	Low-fat milk, fat-free milk, soya milk, evaporated milk, low-fat buttermilk, low-fat plain yoghurt, fat-free plain yoghurt
FAT	Olive oil, canola oil, macadamia nut oil, avocado pears, nuts, seeds, nut butters, low-fat margarine Limit: butter, cream, mayonnaise, salad dressing
CARBOHYDRATE	Whole wheat bread, seeded bread, rye bread, sourdough bread, whole wheat crackers, dried beans such as butter beans, lentils, chickpeas, bulgar wheat, barley, quinoa, brown rice, sweet potatoes, whole wheat pasta, pasta made from durum wheat or semolina, rolled oats, low-fat low-sugar muesli, fiber-rich breakfast cereals
PROTEIN	Lean beef, pork without the fat, skinless chicken, legumes, soya, eggs, fish Limit: lamb/mutton, cheese
FRUIT	Apples, peaches, nectarines, pears, oranges, mandarins, grapefruit, lemons, strawberries, blueberries, cherries
VEGETABLE	Baby marrow, cauliflower, cucumber, gem squash, green beans, mushrooms, tomatoes, carrots, broccoli, cabbage, celery, sweet peppers, lettuce, spinach, onions, garlic

BENEFITS OF EATING A BALANCED DIET FOR DIABETES

Bring together your balanced plate with the recommended foods and you have the beginning of a healthy diet for your whole family.

Aim to eat breakfast, lunch and supper every day. Your meal pattern needs to be aligned with your medication. The goal of the medication is to reduce your blood sugar levels. If you take it and don't eat, you may find yourself experiencing low blood sugar.

When you eat regular meals that contain foods from all of the food groups, it becomes easier to control your blood sugar levels. Meals like this provide your body with enough energy to get you through the day, enough protein to build and repair body tissues, and enough micronutrients to keep you healthy.

Because your blood sugar levels change in relation to what you eat, your diet is the key to diabetes management. A healthy diet can also help you to lose some weight. A lower body weight improves your body's sensitivity to insulin, which improves the way you metabolize sugar.

In some cases, a healthy diet and a regular exercise routine can help you reduce the amount of medication you need to control your blood sugar levels. But, always talk to your doctor before adjusting your medication.

PLAN TO SUCCEED

A newly diagnosed type 2 diabetes condition can be overwhelming. It can feel like you are drowning in conflicting information. Everyone seems to have an opinion. Take your health into your own hands and formulate a plan that works for you. Use the advice from your doctor and dietitian, sit down and figure out how you are going to move forward with your condition.

Your successful management of your type 2 diabetes depends on your commitment. Plan to succeed in taking control of your blood glucose levels. Once you have a plan, it is easier to see your way. The sugary, fatty foods that may have held your attention before become less appealing when your body is receiving all of the energy and nutrition it requires.

Use the comprehensive 21-day meal plan we have compiled to get you started. To go with the plan, we have created 100 delicious and healthy recipes that you and your family will love. Your and your family's health can improve with just a little bit of planning and effort in the kitchen.

We have taken some of the guesswork out of it for you. With recipes like "Chicken Breast In Red Wine Sauce", "Tangy Lemon and Lime Sole Fillet", and "Vegan Thai Red Curry", you are in for healthy, blood-sugar-controlling taste sensations.

28 DAY MEAL PLAN

B. Breakfast   *L.* Lunch   *D.* Dinner

DAY 1	DAY 2	DAY 3	DAY 4	DAY 5
B. Blueberry & Cinnamon Oatmeal Casserole *L.* Pesto Pine Nut, Chicken with Noodles *D.* Sherry Tofu & Spinach Stir-Fry	*B.* Broccoli Purée & Potato Hash Browns *L.* Pistachios & Herb Halibut *D.* Zucchini & Tomato Stew	*B.* Yogurt & Strawberry Pancakes *L.* Garlic Yogurt & Lamb Lettuce Cups *D.* Ham & Cheese Stuffed Chicken Breasts	*B.* Citrus, Poppy & Blueberry Muffins *L.* Smoked Paprika Chicken & Sprouts Bake *D.* Vegetable Lasagna	*B.* Cheesy Broccoli & Mushroom Casserole *L.* Nutty Asparagus Alfredo *D.* Basil Meatball Bake

DAY 6	DAY 7	DAY 8	DAY 9	DAY 10
B. Zucchini & Yellow Pepper Scramble *L.* Citrus Rocket & Vegetable Salad *D.* Creamy Indian Chicken Curry	*B.* ChocoNut Protein Shake *L.* Herb Crusted Turkey Breasts & Veggies *D.* Cauliflower & Rosemary Cottage Pie	*B.* Eggs & Mixed Vegetable Hash *L.* Hawaiian Sushi Tuna *D.* Protein Spinach Casserole	*B.* Orange & Almond Yogurt Parfait *L.* Steak & Guacamole Tortillas *D.* Roasted Cod & French Stew	*B.* ChocChip & Banana Oatmeal Casserole *L.* Italian Goat Cheese Frittata *D.* Sherry Tofu & Spinach Stir-Fry

DAY 11	DAY 12	DAY 13	DAY 14	DAY 15
B. Spicy Pear, Carrot, & Lime Smoothie *L.* Sautéed Spinach & Salmon *D.* Classic French Chicken & Mushroom	*B.* Blueberry & Cinnamon Oatmeal Casserole *L.* Pickled Onion & Pork Lettuce Wraps *D.* Carrot & Lentil Soup	*B.* Vegan Cheese & Vegetable Hash *L.* Spicy Grapefruit & Avocado Salad *D.* Chipotle Cashew Noodles	*B.* ChocoNut Protein Shake *L.* Smoky Melon Salsa & Crabby Cakes *D.* Chicken With Bell Pepper Thyme Sauce	*B.* Citrus, Poppy & Blueberry Muffins *L.* Mixed Greens & Pumpkin Seed Salad *D.* ChocoChili Con Carne

DAY 16	DAY 17	DAY 18	DAY 19	DAY 20
B. Yogurt & Strawberry Pancakes *L.* Fruity Bacon & Veg Bake *D.* Vegetable Lasagna	*B.* Zucchini & Yellow Pepper Scramble *L.* Eggs & Bacon Green Salad *D.* Shrimp & Halibut Sauté	*B.* ChocChip, Banana & Peanut Butter Cup *L.* Cauliflower & Rosemary Cottage Pie *D.* Turkey & Sweet Potato Soup	*B.* Eggs & Mixed Vegetable Hash *L.* Slow-Cooked Orange & Pork Slaw *D.* Cauliflower and Lentil Wraps	*B.* Orange & Almond Yogurt Parfait *L.* Cajun Coconut Cream Prawns *D.* Herbed Chicken & Sweet Potato Bake

DAY 21	DAY 22	DAY 23	DAY 24	DAY 25
B. ChocChip & Banana Oatmeal Casserole *L.* Chicken Breast in Red Wine Sauce *D.* Vegan Thai Red Curry	*B.* Vegan Cheese & Vegetable Hash *L.* Ricotta & Turkey Bell Peppers *D.* Zesty Garlic Sole Fillets	*B.* Apple, Mint & Cucumber Smoothie *L.* Garlic Yogurt & Lamb Lettuce Cups *D.* Zucchini & Tomato Stew	*B.* Cheesy Broccoli & Mushroom Casserole *L.* Italian Goat Cheese Frittata *D.* Basil Meatball Bake	*B.* Broccoli Purée & Potato Hash Browns *L.* Protein Spinach Casserole *D.* Ground Turkey & Lentils Stir-fry

DAY 26	DAY 27	DAY 28		
B. Zucchini & Yellow Pepper Scramble *L.* Nutty Asparagus Alfredo *D.* Fried Haddock & Creamy Summer Sauce	*B.* ChocChip, Banana & Peanut Butter Cup *L.* Tuna, Green Bean & Egg Salad *D.* Orange, Ginger & Honey Lemon Chicken	*B.* Yogurt & Strawberry Pancakes *L.* Quinoa & Beef Soup *D.* Vegetables & Bean Curry		

BREAKFAST

CITRUS, POPPY & BLUEBERRY MUFFINS

COOK TIME: 25 MIN | MAKES: 18

INGREDIENTS:

- Non-stick cooking spray or paper liners
- 2 cups whole wheat pastry flour
- 1 cup almond flour
- ½ cup Splenda sweetener, granulated
- 1 tbsp baking powder
- 2 tsp lemon zest, grated
- ¾ tsp baking soda
- ¾ tsp nutmeg, ground
- 2 tbsp poppy seeds
- Pinch of sea salt, ground

- 2 eggs
- 1 cup plant-based milk, room temperature
- ¾ cup plain low-fat yogurt,
- ½ cup coconut oil, melted
- 1 tbsp lemon juice
- 1 tsp vanilla bean extract
- 1 cup blueberries, frozen or fresh

DIRECTIONS:

1. Preheat the oven to 350°F gas mark 4.

2. Prepare the muffin tin with paper liners or coat with non-stick cooking spray. Set aside.

3. In a stand mixer, mix the whole wheat pastry flour, almond flour, granulated sweetener, baking powder, lemon zest, baking soda, ground nutmeg, poppy seeds, and ground sea salt.

4. In a medium-sized plastic jug, mix the eggs, plant-based milk, low-fat yogurt, melted coconut oil, lemon juice, and vanilla bean extract until well combined.

5. With the mixer on low speed, add the wet ingredients into the dry ingredients until well incorporated.

6. Gently fold in the blueberries with a rubber spatula.

7. Use a medium ice cream scoop to evenly spoon the batter into the prepared muffin tin. Bake for 25 minutes or until the toothpick inserted comes out clean.

8. Place the cooked muffins on a wire rack to cool completely or serve warm with a plant-based butter or organic jam..

Substitution tip: You can use 1 cup all-purpose flour and 1 cup wholewheat flour in place of the 2 cups whole wheat pastry flour.

Tip: You can use the frozen blueberries unthawed in the batter. You can also toss the fresh or frozen blueberries in a little flour to prevent them from sinking to the bottom of the batter.

Per Serving: Calories: 165; Net Carbs: 7g; Protein: 4g; Total Carbs: 18g; Total Fat: 9g

ORANGE & ALMOND YOGURT PARFAIT

PREP TIME: 15 MIN | SERVES: 1

INGREDIENTS:

- ¼ cup unsalted almonds, toasted
- 2 tbsp chia seeds, toasted
- 1 cup plain low-fat yogurt, divided
- 1 medium orange, peeled, chopped, and divided
- 1 tsp honey

DIRECTIONS:

1. In a heavy bottom pan on medium-high heat, add the almonds and the chia seeds and allow to toast.

2. Transfer the toasted almonds and chia seeds into a food processor and pulse 2 to 3 times until chunky.

3. In a dessert bowl or mason jar, add half the plain yogurt, half the chopped orange, and half of the toasted almonds and chia seeds. Repeat for the last layer and drizzle with honey.

4. Keep it in the fridge or serve immediately.

Substitution tip: Fresh berries or bananas are also good ingredients to use in place of the oranges.

Per Serving: Calories: 397; Protein: 22g; Total Carbs: 26g; Total Fat: 27g

BLUEBERRY & CINNAMON OATMEAL CASSEROLE

COOK TIME: 35 MIN | SERVES: 6

INGREDIENTS:

- Non-stick cooking spray or vegan butter
- 2 cups rolled oats or muesli
- ¼ cup unsweetened coconut, flaked
- 1 tsp baking powder
- ½ tsp cinnamon, ground
- ¼ tsp Himalayan salt, ground
- 2 cups plant-based milk
- ¼ cup vegan butter, melted
- 1 large egg
- 1 tsp vanilla bean extract
- 2 cups fresh or frozen blueberries, divided
- ⅛ cup pecans, chopped
- 1 tsp fresh mint leaves, chopped

DIRECTIONS:

1. Preheat the oven to 350°F gas mark 4.

2. Prepare the casserole dish by lightly coating it with vegan butter or non-stick cooking spray. Set aside.

3. In a large bowl, combine the rolled oats or muesli, flaked coconut, baking powder, cinnamon, and ground Himalayan salt. Place to one side.

4. In a medium plastic jug, whisk together the plant-based milk, melted vegan butter, egg, and vanilla bean extract until well combined.

5. In the prepared casserole dish, add half of the rolled oat mixture and top it with half of the blueberries. Spoon the remailing rolled oat mixture onto the berries and add the rest of the blueberries on top.

6. Gently pour the wet ingredients evenly over the dry ingredients, tap the dish lightly on the counter to spread the liquid.

7. Bake uncovered for 35 minutes or until the oats are tender.

8. Garnish with chopped pecan nut and chopped mint leaves. Serve immediately.

Per Serving: Calories: 295; Net Carbs: 11g; Protein: 10g; Total Carbs: 27g; Total Fat: 17g

CHOCCHIP & BANANA OATMEAL CASSEROLE

COOK TIME: 30 MIN | SERVES: 6

INGREDIENTS:

- Non-stick cooking spray
- 1 ripe banana, mashed
- 1 cup unsweetened cashew milk
- 2 eggs, large
- 1 tsp vanilla bean extract
- Pinch of sea salt, ground
- 2 cups rolled oats or muesli
- ½ cup almond flour
- 1 tsp baking powder
- ¼ cup dark chocolate chips
- ¼ cup plain yogurt

DIRECTIONS:

1. Set the oven temperature to 350°F gas mark 4. Spray a casserole dish with non-stick cooking spray and set it to one side.
2. In a large bowl, add the mashed banana, unsweetened cashew milk, eggs, vanilla bean extract, and salt, mix until incorporated. Add the rolled oats or muesli, almond flour, and baking powder and mix well.
3. Pour the mixture into the prepared casserole dish and scatter the chocolate chips on top.
4. Bake for 30 minutes or until golden.
5. Cut and serve with yogurt.

Ingredient tip: Use 55% dark chocolate if you do not want a bitter cocoa flavor.

Substitution tip: Use chopped apples covered in cinnamon in place of the banana.

Per Serving: Calories: 245; Protein: 9g; Total Carbs: 30g; Total Fat: 10g

ZUCCHINI & YELLOW PEPPER SCRAMBLE

COOK TIME: 10 MIN | SERVES: 4

INGREDIENTS:

- 1 tsp olive oil
- 1 spring onion, diced
- ½ yellow bell pepper, cut into cubes
- ½ zucchini, cut into cubes
- 8 large eggs, beaten
- 1 tomato, seeded and cut into cubes
- 2 tsp fresh oregano, diced finely
- Himalayan pink salt, ground
- Black pepper, ground

DIRECTIONS:

1. Heat a heavy bottom pan over medium heat and add the olive oil and cook until hot.
2. Toss in the diced spring onion, cubed yellow bell pepper, and the cubed zucchini, fry for 5 minutes until tender.
3. Add the beaten eggs and using a spatula or fork, scramble the egg mixture for 5 minutes or until the eggs are cooked through.
4. Remove the pan off the heat and add the cubed tomato and diced oregano, mix to combine.
5. Season with ground Himalayan pink salt and ground black pepper and serve warm..

Ingredient tip: Smoked sea salt will add a smoky flavor to the dish.

Per Serving: Calories: 196; Net Carbs: 2g; Protein: 13g; Total Carbs: 4g; Total Fat: 11g

YOGURT & STRAWBERRY PANCAKES

COOK TIME: 20 MIN | SERVES: 5

INGREDIENTS:

- 1 ½ cups almond milk
- 3 eggs
- 1 tsp olive oil, extra for frying
- 1 cup buckwheat flour, sifted
- ½ cup whole wheat flour, sifted
- ½ cup low-fat yogurt, plain
- 1 cup strawberries, sliced
- 1 cup blueberries, halved
- honey

DIRECTIONS:

1. In a large bowl, using a hand mixer, beat the almond milk, eggs, and 1 tsp of olive oil until incorporated.

2. Add the sifted buckwheat flour and sifted whole wheat flour into the wet ingredients. Mix until smooth.

3. Allow to rest for 2 hours before cooking.

4. With a heavy bottom pan or crêpe pan on medium heat, lightly coat the bottom with the extra olive oil.

5. Pour a ¼ cup or a small ladle of batter into the pan and swirl it around in a circle until it covers the bottom of the pan, cook for 1 minute and turn it over until golden.

6. Move the pancake onto a plate and repeat with the remaining batter.

7. Add 1 tbsp of plain yogurt onto half of each pancake and add the sliced strawberries and halved blueberries on top of the yogurt fold the pancake and drizzle with honey.

Per Serving (2 pancakes): Calories: 329; Net Carbs: 11g; Protein: 16g; Total Carbs: 54g; Total Fat: 7g

EGGS & MIXED VEGETABLE HASH

COOK TIME: 15 – 20 MIN | SERVES: 4

INGREDIENTS:

- 1 broccoli head, cut into florets
- 1 medium red and green bell peppers, sliced
- 1 small onion, thinly sliced
- ¼ cup fresh mixed herbs, roughly chopped
- 3 tbsp coconut oil, melted and divided
- Himalayan Pink salt, ground
- Black pepper, ground
- Paprika spice, ground
- 8 large eggs

DIRECTIONS:

1. Heat the oven to 425°F gas mark 7. Line the baking sheet with aluminum foil.

2. In a large bowl, add the broccoli florets, sliced red and green bell peppers, sliced onion, and chopped mixed herbs. Drizzle with 2 tbsp of melted coconut oil and season with ground Himalayan Pink salt, ground black pepper, and ground paprika. Toss to combine.

3. Place the baking sheet into the preheated oven and roast the vegetables for 15 to 20 minutes until they are cooked and slightly browned.

4. While the vegetables are cooking, heat a large heavy bottom pan over medium heat and add the remaining 1 tbsp coconut oil until hot.

5. Fry the eggs until they reach your desired consistency.

6. Divide the roast vegetables onto 4 plates and add the fried eggs on top. Serve immediately.

Ingredient tip: Here are some fresh herbs that you can use in this recipe, parsley, basil, thyme, rosemary, spring onion, chives, and sage.

Per Serving: Calories: 269; Net Carbs: 8g; Protein: 14g; Total Carbs: 12g; Total Fat: 20g

CHEESY BROCCOLI & MUSHROOM CASSEROLE

COOK TIME: 40 MIN | SERVES: 4

INGREDIENTS:

- 2 tbsp olive oil
- 1 cup portobello mushrooms, sliced
- ½ onion, finely chopped
- 1 tsp garlic, crushed
- 1 cup broccoli, cut into small florets
- 8 large eggs
- ¼ cup almond milk
- 1 tbsp fresh basil, finely chopped
- 1 cup vegan cheese, grated
- Himalayan Pink salt, ground
- Black pepper, ground

DIRECTIONS:

1. Heat the oven to 375°F gas mark 5.

2. Using a cast-iron pan over medium heat, cook the olive oil until hot.

3. Fry the sliced portobello mushrooms, finely chopped onion, and crushed garlic for 5 minutes or until browned.

4. Add the broccoli florets and sauté for a further 5 minutes and remove from the heat.

5. In a small jug, add the eggs, almond milk, and finely chopped basil and whisk to combine.

6. Gently pour the egg mixture over the vegetables and sprinkle with grated vegan cheese.

7. Bake uncovered for 30 minutes or until the eggs have puffed up.

8. Season with ground Himalayan Pink salt and ground black pepper. Serve.

Substitution tip: You can use any dairy cheese in this recipe.

Ingredient tip: The best vegan cheese to use is a coconut oil-based one. The texture of the coconut oil-based cheese is smooth and creamy. You can mix the recipe up with different vegetables and add some fresh herbs into the dish.

Per Serving: Calories: 273; Net Carbs: 3g; Protein: 21g; Total Carbs: 5g; Total Fat: 19g

BROCCOLI PURÉE & POTATO HASH BROWNS

COOK TIME: 25 MIN | SERVES: 4

INGREDIENTS:

- 1 cup broccoli, cut into florets
- Sea salt, ground
- ½ lb. peeled russet potatoes, grated and patted dry
- ¼ onion, finely chopped
- 1 tsp olive oil
- 1 tsp fresh thyme, chopped
- Black pepper, ground
- Non-stick cooking spray

DIRECTIONS:

1. Put the broccoli florets in a medium-sized pot and add a pinch of ground sea salt. Boil for 2 to 3 minutes until tender.

2. Allow it to drain completely, making sure all excess water is gone. Transfer into a food processor and purée. Set aside.

3. Place the grated potatoes, finely chopped onion, olive oil, and chopped fresh thyme in a large bowl. Season with ground sea salt and ground black pepper and mix.

4. Place a large heavy bottom pan over medium heat and spray with non-stick cooking spray.

5. Add a ¼ cup of the potato mixture per hash brown, press down with a spatula, and cook for 5 to 7 minutes until the bottom is firm and golden. Flip the hash brown over and cook for 5 more minutes until completely cooked through and golden.

6. Remove and repeat with the remaining potato mixture.

7. Serve it with the homemade broccoli purée.

Ingredient tip: You can use unsweetened applesauce in place of the broccoli purée.

Per Serving: Calories: 106; Net Carbs: 7g; Protein: 1g; Total Carbs: 18g; Total Fat: 3g

VEGAN CHEESE & VEGETABLE HASH

COOK TIME: 20 MIN | SERVES: 4

INGREDIENTS:

- 3 tbsp coconut oil
- 4 cups brussels sprouts, shredded
- ½ cup onion, finely chopped
- ½ cup red bell pepper, cut into cubes
- 1 tbsp garlic, crushed
- 8 large eggs
- ½ cup vegan cheese, grated
- ¼ tsp sea salt, ground
- ½ tsp black pepper, ground
- ¼ cup fresh parsley, finely chopped

DIRECTIONS:

1. Place the coconut oil in a large heavy bottom pan on medium heat until hot. Add the shredded brussels sprouts, finely chopped onion, cubed red bell pepper, and crushed garlic. Cook for 10 minutes until the vegetables are tender and lightly browned.

2. Crack the eggs over the vegetables and sprinkle with grated vegan cheese and season to taste.

3. Put the heat on low and cover with a lid. Cook for a further 5 to 6 minutes, or until your desired egg consistency and the cheese has melted.

4. Serve onto 4 plates and garnish with finely chopped parsley..

Substitution tip: You can use dairy cheddar cheese in this recipe.

Ingredient tip: The best vegan cheese to use is a coconut oil-based one. The texture of the coconut oil-based cheese is smooth and creamy and dairy-free.

Per Serving: Calories: 336; Net Carbs: 8g; Protein: 18g; Total Carbs: 12g; Total Fat: 24g

CHOCONUT PROTEIN SHAKE

PREP TIME: 2 MIN | SERVES: 1

INGREDIENTS:

- 1 cup unsweetened almond milk
- 1 cup ice cubes
- 2 tbsp organic peanut butter
- 1 scoop vegan protein powder, chocolate

DIRECTIONS:

1. Place the unsweetened almond milk, ice cubes organic peanut butter, and the vegan chocolate protein shake in a blender.

2. Mix until smooth, scraping the sides if needed.

Substitution tip: You can use any plant-based milk for this recipe.

Per Serving: Calories: 389; Net Carbs: 17g; Protein: 26g; Total Carbs: 19g; Total Fat: 25g

APPLE, MINT & CUCUMBER SMOOTHIE

PREP TIME: 5 MIN | SERVES: 2

INGREDIENTS:

- 2 English cucumbers, chopped
- 1 cup low-fat, plain yogurt
- 1 green apple, core removed and chopped
- ¼ cup fresh mint leaves
- 1 lemon, juiced
- 3 ice cubes

DIRECTIONS:

1. Add the chopped cucumbers, low-fat plain yogurt, chopped apple, fresh mint leaves, lemon juice, and ice cubes in a blender. Mix until smooth and no chunks remain.

2. Pour into two glasses and serve.

Nutrition tip: Mint leaves help to reduce the risk of diabetes. It also relieves indigestion.

Ingredient tip: Using a tart apple like Granny Smith, is the better choice.

Per Serving: Calories: 136; Net Carbs: 18g; Protein: 7g; Total Carbs: 26g; Total Fat: 2g

SPICY PEAR, CARROT, & LIME SMOOTHIE

PREP TIME: 10 MIN | SERVES: 2

INGREDIENTS:

- 2 medium-sized carrots, peeled and grated
- 1 medium ripe pear, cored and chopped
- 2 tsp fresh ginger, grated
- 1 lime, juiced, and zested
- 1 cup water
- ½ tsp cinnamon, ground
- ¼ tsp nutmeg, ground

DIRECTIONS:

1. Place the grated carrots, chopped pear, grated ginger, lime juice and zest, water, ground cinnamon, and ground nutmeg into a blender. Blend until completely smooth.

2. Fill two glasses with the mixture and serve cold.

Nutrition tip: Cinnamon helps with blood sugar control and has antibacterial and anti-inflammatory effects. Ginger lowers your blood sugar and assists with chronic indigestion.

Per Serving: Calories: 74; Net Carbs: 11g; Protein: 1g; Total Carbs: 19g; Total Fat: 0g

CHOCCHIP, BANANA & PEANUT BUTTER CUP

PREP TIME: 5 MIN | SERVES 1

INGREDIENTS:

- ½ cup low-fat yogurt, plain
- Pinch of Stevia sweetener
- 2 tbsp organic peanut butter, smooth
- 1 tbsp dark chocolate chips
- Pinch of sea salt, ground
- 1 tbsp salted peanuts, roughly chopped
- ½ banana, chopped

DIRECTIONS:

1. In a dessert bowl, combine the low-fat yogurt and a pinch of stevia.

2. Add the organic peanut butter, dark chocolate chips, and the chopped banana and mix to combine.

3. Sprinkle with a pinch of ground sea salt and the roughly chopped peanuts.

Ingredient tip: Use 55% dark chocolate if you do not want a bitter cocoa flavor.

Per Serving: Calories: 315; Net Carbs: 15g; Protein: 15g; Total Carbs: 18g; Total Fat: 25g

SALADS & SIDES

MIXED GREENS & PUMPKIN SEED SALAD

PREP TIME: 15 MIN | SERVES: 4

INGREDIENTS:

FOR THE DRESSING:
- ½ cup olive oil
- ¼ cup lemon juice, freshly squeezed
- 1 tsp garlic, minced
- Sea salt, ground
- Black pepper, ground

FOR THE SALAD:
- 10 oz leafy greens, salad mix
- 2 avocados, chopped
- 1 cup cucumber, chopped
- 1 cup carrots, grated
- 1 cup celery, diced
- ½ cup pumpkin seeds, toasted

DIRECTIONS:

FOR THE DRESSING:

1. In a small jug, mix the olive oil, fresh lemon juice, and minced garlic. Season with salt and pepper.

FOR THE SALAD:

2. In a large serving bowl, add the mixed leafy greens, chopped avocados, chopped cucumber, grated carrots, diced celery, and toasted pumpkin seeds.

3. Drizzle the homemade dressing and toss to combine.

4. Serve or refrigerate for later.

Substitution tip: You can use green bell pepper in place of the celery.

Per Serving: Calories: 489; Net Carbs: 6g; Protein: 7g; Total Carbs: 14g; Total Fat: 45g

EGGS & BACON GREEN SALAD

COOK TIME: 20 MIN | SERVES: 4

INGREDIENTS:

FOR THE SALAD:
- 4 large eggs
- 1 lb. bacon, chopped
- 10 oz baby spinach, rinsed and dried
- 10 oz rocket, rinsed and dried
- ½ cup red onion, thinly sliced
- Ice in a bowl

FOR THE DRESSING:
- 3 tbsp avocado oil
- 2 tbsp balsamic vinegar
- ½ tbsp garlic, minced
- Himalayan Pink Salt
- Black pepper, ground

DIRECTIONS:

FOR THE SALAD:

1. In a medium pot add the eggs and fill it with cold water and bring to a boil over high heat. Cook for 7 to 8 minutes and remove from the heat and then transfer into an ice water bath. This allows the eggs to be peeled easier. Remove the eggshells and cut them into slices. Set aside for later.

2. In a heavy bottom pan, over medium heat, cook the bacon for 8 to 10 minutes, turning it until crispy. Drain the bacon on paper towels and keep the bacon grease in the pan for the dressing.

FOR THE DRESSING:

3. In a small bowl, combine the olive oil, balsamic vinegar, minced garlic, and 3 tbsp of reserved bacon grease. Season to taste.

4. Divide the dried spinach and dried rocket between 4 bowls, sprinkle the chopped bacon, sliced red onion, and sliced eggs.

5. Drizzle with the homemade salad dressing.

Per Serving: Calories: 589; Net Carbs: 4g; Protein: 36g; Total Carbs: 6g; Total Fat: 47g

CITRUS ROCKET & VEGETABLE SALAD

COOK TIME: 1 HOUR | SERVES: 4 – 6

INGREDIENTS:

- 1 medium eggplant, cut into large cubes
- 2 medium red bell peppers, cut into chunks
- 2 medium courgettes, cut into large cubes
- 2 tsp garlic, minced
- ½ cup avocado oil
- 2 medium lemons, juiced
- 1 tbsp lemon zest, divided
- 1 tsp sea salt, ground
- ½ tsp black pepper, ground
- 4 rosemary sprigs, rinsed
- 3 cups rocket, rinsed and dried
- ½ cup pine nuts, toasted

DIRECTIONS:

1. Preheat the oven to 350°F gas mark 4. Line a baking sheet with aluminum foil.

2. In a large bowl, add the cubed eggplant, red bell pepper chunks, cubed courgettes, minced garlic, avocado oil, fresh lemon juice, half the lemon zest, ground sea salt, and ground black pepper and mix.

3. Spread the mixture into a single layer and place the rinsed rosemary sprigs on top.

4. Bake for 40 minutes and then remove the baking sheet from the oven.

5. Discard the rosemary sprigs and using a spatula, turn and mix the vegetables. Return the baking sheet to the oven for another 20 minutes or until vegetables are tender.

6. Transfer the roasted vegetables onto a large platter and top them with the dried rocket, remaining lemon zest, and pine nuts.

Substitution tip: You can use oranges in place of the lemons.

Per Serving: Calories: 201; Protein: 6g; Total Carbs: 21g; Total Fat: 13g

TUNA, GREEN BEAN & EGG SALAD

COOK TIME: 20 MIN | SERVES: 4

INGREDIENTS:

- 8 oz green beans, washed and trimmed
- 8 large eggs
- 8 oz fresh tuna fillets, rinsed and dried
- 4 tbsp olive oil, divided
- Sea salt, ground
- Black pepper, ground
- 8 cups mixed lettuce leaves
- 1 cup cherry tomatoes, washed and halved
- 1 cup marinated artichoke hearts, quartered and drained
- ½ cup black olives, pitted
- ½ lemon, juiced

DIRECTIONS:

1. In a large pot, add water and salt and bring it to a boil and fill a separate bowl with ice water.

2. Place the trimmed green beans into the boiling water and cook for 3 minutes, or until bright green and tender. Using a slotted spoon transfer the cooked green beans into the ice water bowl briefly.

3. With the pot of water already at a gentle boil, add the eggs. Cook for 10 minutes, then transfer into the ice water bath.

4. Heat a large heavy bottom pan on medium-high heat until hot.

5. Coat the dried tuna fillets with 1 tbsp of olive oil, and season generously with salt and pepper.

6. Place the tuna fillet in the hot pan, and sear for 2 minutes on each side for medium-rare. The fish will still be deep pink in the center.

7. Put the tuna fillet onto a cutting board and cut it into thick pieces.

8. Peel the cooked eggs and slice them into quarters.

9. When ready to serve, divide the mixed lettuce, quartered eggs, tuna fillet, halved cherry tomatoes, drained and quartered artichoke hearts, pitted olives, and cooked green beans among 4 serving dishes. Finish off by drizzling with the remaining 3 tbsp of olive oil and lemon juice..

Substitution tip: You can replace the artichoke hearts with steamed asparagus or brussels sprouts.

Per Serving: Calories: 431; Net Carbs: 9g; Protein: 28g; Total Carbs: 15g; Total Fat: 30g

PARMESAN & COURGETTE FRITTERS

COOK TIME: 15 MIN | SERVES: 4

INGREDIENTS:

- 4 cups courgette, julienned
- 2 tsp sea salt, ground
- ½ cup whole wheat flour
- 2 large eggs
- ½ cup vegan parmesan cheese, grated
- 12 tbsp mayonnaise, remove 2 tbsp into a bowl
- 6 tsp minced garlic, divided
- 2 tbsp olive oil
- 1 tbsp lemon juice
- ½ tsp lemon zest
- Black pepper, ground

DIRECTIONS:

1. Place a colander over a large bowl and put in the julienned courgettes. Sprinkle with ground sea salt, mix well, and let them stand for 10 minutes until the liquid drains. Gently squeeze the julienned courgettes to remove any extra liquid.

2. In a large bowl, add the julienned courgettes, whole wheat flour, eggs, grated vegan parmesan cheese, 2 tbsp mayonnaise, half of the minced garlic, and mix well.

3. Place paper towels on a large plate to absorb the oil from the fritters.

4. Heat the olive oil in a heavy bottom pan over medium-high heat. Drop the courgette mixture into the pan, one spoonful at a time, and press down with a spatula to form a patty.

5. Cook the fritters for 3 minutes on each side, until lightly browned. Place the cooked fritters onto the prepared plate with the paper towels to drain.

6. In a small bowl, add the remaining mayonnaise, minced garlic, lemon zest, lemon juice, and mix well to make a dipping sauce. Season with ground sea salt and ground black pepper.

7. Serve the fritters warm with the dipping sauce on the side.

Substitution tip: you can use a non-vegan parmesan cheese for this recipe, or sharp cheddar cheese.

Per Serving: Calories: 499; Net Carbs: 6g; Protein: 11g; Total Carbs: 8g; Total Fat: 47g

ENDIVE & SWEET POTATO BAKE

COOK TIME: 45 MIN | SERVES: 4

INGREDIENTS:

- Non-stick cooking spray
- 2 endives, leaves separated and divided
- 2 orange sweet potatoes, peeled and thinly sliced
- Black pepper, ground
- 1 tbsp fennel seeds, ground
- ½ tsp cinnamon, ground
- ¼ tsp nutmeg, ground
- 1 cup vegetable broth

DIRECTIONS:

1. Heat the oven to 375°F gas mark 5. Prepare a deep baking dish by coating it with non-stick cooking spray.

2. Cover the bottom of the baking dish with half the endive leaves and layer half the thinly sliced sweet potatoes on top.

3. Sprinkle the ground black pepper, ground fennel seeds, and half the ground cinnamon and ground nutmeg on top of the potatoes.

4. Continue to do this for the next few layers, until all the endive leaves, sliced sweet potatoes, ground cinnamon, ground fennel seeds, and ground nutmeg is used.

5. Add the vegetable broth and cover the deep baking dish with aluminum foil.

6. Bake for 45 minutes until the vegetables are tender.

7. Serve hot.

Substitution tip: You can use white sweet potatoes or yams for this recipe, and you can replace the endives with 1 fennel bulb sliced.

Per Serving: Calories: 153; Net Carbs: 1g; Protein: 3g; Total Carbs: 33g; Total Fat: 2g

SPICY GRAPEFRUIT & AVOCADO SALAD

PREP TIME: 10 MIN | SERVES: 4

INGREDIENTS:

- 1 head lettuce, torn into small pieces
- 2 ripe avocados, pitted and cubed
- 2 grapefruits, peeled and cut into wedges
- 1 tsp grapefruit zest
- 2 tbsp olive oil
- ¼ tsp red pepper flakes
- Sea salt

DIRECTIONS:

1. Place the torn lettuce leaves onto a serving platter.
2. Scatter the cubed avocado and peeled grapefruit wedges.
3. Sprinkle the grapefruit zest over the salad.
4. Drizzle with olive oil and season with red pepper flakes and sea salt.

Per Serving: Calories: 269; Net Carbs: 14g; Protein: 3g; Total Carbs: 23g; Total Fat: 21g

GREEN BEANS, BLUE CHEESE & ALMONDS

COOK TIME: 5 MIN | SERVES: 4

INGREDIENTS:

- 1 tbsp avocado oil
- 8 oz green beans, rinsed and ends trimmed
- ¼ cup sliced almonds, toasted
- 1 lemon, juiced
- ¼ cup blue cheese, crumbled
- Himalayan Pink salt, ground
- Black pepper, ground

DIRECTIONS:

1. Heat the avocado oil in a heavy bottom pan over medium-high heat, until hot. Add the rinsed and trimmed green beans and cook stirring for 5 minutes, until tender.
2. Add the toasted sliced almonds, lemon juice, and mix.
3. Divide the green beans onto 4 plates and top with crumbled blue cheese and season with Himalayan Pink salt and ground black pepper.

Substitution tip: You can use feta cheese in place of the blue cheese.

Per Serving: Calories: 121; Net Carbs: 3g; Protein: 4g; Total Carbs: 6g; Total Fat: 9g

MOZZARELLA & TOMATO SALAD

PREP TIME: 10 MIN | SERVES: 4

INGREDIENTS:

- 2 (4 oz) mozzarella cheese, cut into thick slices
- 2 large tomatoes, cut into thick slices
- 2 tbsp balsamic vinegar
- 2 tbsp olive oil
- 4 basil leaves, finely chopped
- Himalayan Pink salt
- Black pepper, ground

DIRECTIONS:

1. Layer the thickly sliced mozzarella and the thickly sliced tomatoes together, overlapping each other slightly on individual serving plates.

2. Carefully drizzle the balsamic vinegar and olive oil and top with the finely chopped basil leaves. Season with Himalayan pink salt and ground black pepper.

Per Serving: Calories: 233; Net Carbs: 2g; Protein: 11g; Total Carbs: 3g; Total Fat: 21g

ALMOND & SESAME BOK CHOY

COOK TIME: 7 MIN | SERVES: 4

INGREDIENTS:

- 2 tsp sesame oil
- 2 lbs. Bok choy, rinsed and quartered
- 2 tsp low-salt soy sauce
- ¼ tsp red pepper flakes
- ½ cup sliced almonds, toasted
- 2 tbsp sesame seeds, toasted

DIRECTIONS:

1. In a large heavy bottom pan over high heat add the sliced almonds and allow to toast. Remove the almonds and repeat with the sesame seeds. Set aside.

2. In the same pan on medium heat, heat the sesame oil until hot. Fry the quartered Bok choy for 5 minutes, until tender.

3. Add the low-salt soy sauce and red pepper flakes and fry for 2 minutes, until incorporated.

4. Transfer the Bok choy into a large serving bowl and top with the toasted, sliced almonds and toasted sesame seeds and serve.

Substitution tip: You can use any leafy greens like kale, cabbage, and spinach.

Per Serving: Calories: 119; Net Carbs: 3g; Protein: 6g; Total Carbs: 8g; Total Fat: 8g

SULTANA & PUMPKIN SEED WILD RICE

COOK TIME: 45 MIN | SERVES: 4

INGREDIENTS:

- 1 tbsp olive oil
- ½ red onion, finely chopped
- 2½ cups no sodium chicken broth
- 1 cup wild rice, rinsed and drained
- Pinch sea salt
- ½ cup pumpkin seeds, toasted
- ½ cup sultanas
- 1 tsp basil, chopped

DIRECTIONS:

1. In a heavy bottom pan over medium-high heat, add the olive oil and cook until hot.

2. Fry the finely chopped onion for 3 minutes until translucent.

3. Add the no sodium chicken broth and allow to boil.

4. Add the wild rice and sea salt and reduce the heat to low. Cover and simmer the rice for 40 minutes until fully cooked.

5. Drain excess broth, if necessary, and stir in the toasted pumpkin seeds, sultanas, and chopped basil.

6. Serve hot.

Substitution tip: You can substitute the wild rice with long-grain brown rice.

Per Serving: Calories: 258; Net Carbs: 4g; Protein: 11g; Total Carbs: 37g; Total Fat: 9g

PARMESAN & HERB SPAGHETTI SQUASH

COOK TIME: 60 MIN | SERVES 4

INGREDIENTS:

- 1 (2 lb.) spaghetti squash, cut lengthwise
- Sea salt, ground
- Black pepper, ground
- 3 tbsp olive oil, divided
- 1 tbsp fresh basil, finely diced
- 1 tbsp fresh parsley, finely diced
- 1 tbsp fresh rosemary, finely diced
- 2 tsp garlic, minced
- ¼ cup vegan parmesan cheese, grated

DIRECTIONS:

1. Turn on the oven and heat to 400°F or gas mark 6. Use aluminum foil to cover the baking sheet.

2. Season the halved spaghetti squash with ground sea salt and ground black pepper and drizzle with 1 tbsp olive oil.

3. Put the spaghetti squash, cut side down, on the baking sheet, and bake for 50 to 60 minutes, until tender. Let cool for a few minutes.

4. Use a fork to scrape the spaghetti squash strands into a large serving bowl and add the remaining 2 tbsp olive oil, finely diced basil, parsley, rosemary, minced garlic, and mix to combine. Season with ground sea salt and ground black pepper.

5. Top with grated vegan parmesan cheese and serve.

Substitution tip: You can use julienned courgettes in place of the spaghetti squash.

Ingredient tip: You can use any hard white cheese for this recipe. Using vegan cheese will make this a dairy-free dish.

Per Serving: Calories: 174; Net Carbs: 16g; Protein: 4g; Total Carbs: 17g; Total Fat: 10g

ROSEMARY GRILLED VEGETABLES

COOK TIME: 8 MIN | SERVES: 4

INGREDIENTS:

- 2 tsp olive oil
- 2 peeled carrots, sliced
- 1 small broccoli head, broken into florets
- 1 small cauliflower head, broken into florets
- 1 medium red bell pepper, cut into strips
- 1 cup green beans, trim ends
- 1 tbsp rosemary, finely chopped
- Himalayan Pink salt, ground
- Black pepper, ground

DIRECTIONS:

1. Place a large grill pan over medium heat and add the olive oil.

2. Fry the sliced carrots, broccoli florets, and cauliflower florets for 6 minutes, or until tender.

3. Mix in the bell pepper strips, trimmed green beans, finely chopped rosemary, and grill for 2 minutes stirring occasionally.

4. Season with ground Himalayan Pink salt and ground black pepper and serve warm.

Per Serving: Calories: 106; Net Carbs: 7g; Protein: 6g; Total Carbs: 18g; Total Fat: 3g

CRANBERRY & CURRIED CAULIFLOWER ROAST

COOK TIME: 20 – 25 MIN | SERVES: 4

INGREDIENTS:

- 1 head cauliflower, cut into florets
- 2 tbsp olive oil
- 1 tbsp curry powder
- ¼ cup cranberries, dried
- ½ tsp Himalayan pink salt

DIRECTIONS:

1. Heat the oven to 375°F, gas mark 5.

2. In a large mixing bowl, using your hands, mix the cauliflower florets and the olive oil, until fully coated.

3. Mix in the curry powder, dried cranberries and Himalayan pink salt and toss to combine.

4. Transfer the cauliflower mixture into a deep ovenproof dish, and bake for 20 to 25 minutes, until the cauliflower is fully cooked and lightly browned.

Ingredient tip: Dried cranberries are considered to be a superfood because of their high nutrient and antioxidant properties.

Per Serving: Calories: 100; Net Carbs: 5g; Protein: 3g; Total Carbs: 9g; Total Fat: 7g

POULTRY

CHICKEN BREAST IN RED WINE SAUCE

COOK TIME: 15 MIN | SERVES: 2

INGREDIENTS:

- 4 chicken breasts, skinless and boneless
- 1 tbsp avocado oil
- Himalayan pink salt, ground
- Black pepper, ground
- 2 medium courgettes, cut into bite-size pieces
- 1 tsp fresh thyme
- ¼ cup dry red wine

DIRECTIONS:

1. Butterfly the chicken breasts and pat dry with paper towels. Season with ground Himalayan pink salt and ground black pepper.

2. In a heavy bottom pan on medium heat, add the avocado oil until hot.

3. Gently place the chicken breasts into the hot pan, and fry for 4 to 5 minutes, then turn the chicken breasts over and cook for another 4 minutes.

4. Place the chicken breasts onto a cutting board to rest.

5. In the same pan, add the bite-size courgettes and fresh thyme, and fry for 2 to 3 minutes, until browned and al dente.

6. Portion the courgettes between 2 serving plates and place the chicken breasts on top.

7. Add the dry red wine into the same pan, and simmer gently for 2 minutes, until reduced by half. Use a wooden spoon to scrape any browned bits from the bottom of the pan.

8. Pour the dry red wine reduction over the chicken breasts and courgettes.

Per Serving: Calories: 377; Net Carbs: 6g; Protein: 47g; Total Carbs: 8g; Total Fat: 16g

CLASSIC FRENCH CHICKEN & MUSHROOM

COOK TIME: 20 MIN | SERVES: 2

INGREDIENTS:

- 4 chicken thighs, skinless and deboned
- 1 tbsp olive oil
- Himalayan pink salt, ground
- Black pepper, ground
- 2 cups button mushrooms, sliced
- 1 small onion, minced
- 2 tbsp semi-sweet red wine
- ¼ cup imitation cream or coconut cream

DIRECTIONS:

1. Using paper towels, dry the chicken thighs completely and season with Himalayan pink salt and ground black pepper.

2. In a large heavy bottom pan, over medium-high heat, cook the olive oil until hot.

3. Gently place the chicken thighs into the hot pan, and fry for 4 to 5 minutes. Turn them over and fry for a further 4 minutes until cooked through.

4. Place the cooked chicken thighs onto a cutting board to rest.

5. In the same pan, add the sliced mushrooms, and fry for 2 minutes stirring occasionally, until lightly browned.

6. Add the minced onion and cook for 2 minutes until translucent.

7. Add the port wine and scrape the bottom of the pan with a wooden spoon to loosen the browned bits. Cook for 2 minutes, until the wine has reduced.

8. Pour in the imitation cream and mix. Add the cooked chicken thighs and any accumulated juices and simmer gently for 2 minutes.

Ingredient tip: You can use heavy cream in place of the imitation cream. Imitation cream and coconut cream are dairy-free alternatives used in this recipe.

Substitution tip: You can substitute the creams for cream cheese or cottage cheese.

Per Serving: Calories: 325; Net Carbs: 3g; Protein: 36g; Total Carbs: 4g; Total Fat: 20g

SMOKED PAPRIKA CHICKEN & SPROUTS BAKE

COOK TIME: 45 MIN | SERVES: 4

INGREDIENTS:

- 4 chicken drumsticks
- Himalayan Pink salt, ground
- Black pepper, ground
- 1 lb. sprouts, trimmed
- ¼ cup avocado oil, extra for drizzling
- 4 tbsp plant-based butter
- 1 tbsp smoked paprika
- ¼ cup parsley, finely chopped
- 4½ tsp garlic, minced

DIRECTIONS:

1. Heat the oven to 375°F gas mark 5. Cover a baking sheet with aluminum foil.

2. Season the chicken drumsticks with ground Himalayan pink salt and ground black pepper. Set aside.

3. Put the sprouts onto the prepared baking sheet and season them with ground Himalayan Pink salt and ground black pepper. Drizzle with avocado oil and toss to combine.

4. In a small saucepan over medium heat, add the plant-based butter, avocado oil, smoked paprika, finely chopped parsley, minced garlic, and cook for 1 to 2 minutes stirring to combine.

5. In a large bowl, add the seasoned chicken drumsticks, and pour the butter mixture over the chicken drumsticks, and toss to coat. Place the chicken drumsticks onto the baking sheet, scattering them around the sprouts. Drizzle any remaining butter mixture over the chicken drumsticks and sprouts.

6. Bake for 35 to 45 minutes, until the chicken drumsticks and sprouts are fully cooked.

Per Serving: Calories: 512; Net Carbs: 8g; Protein: 26g; Total Carbs: 12g; Total Fat: 40g

CITRUSY VEG CHICKEN ROAST

COOK TIME: 2 HOURS | SERVES: 4

INGREDIENTS:

- 2 tbsp rosemary, thyme, and oregano, stems removed
- 1 orange, zested, and cut into quarters
- 12 garlic cloves, peeled and divided
- 3 tbsp olive oil, extra for drizzling
- 3 tbsp plant-based butter
- 2 tsp Himalayan pink salt, ground and divided
- 2½ tsp black pepper, ground and divided
- 2 medium cauliflower heads, cut into florets
- 12 oz carrots, peeled and thickly sliced
- 1 (6 – 7 lb.) whole chicken

DIRECTIONS:

1. Preheat the oven to 400°F gas mark 6. Place a deep roasting pan to the side.

2. In a food chopper, add the rosemary, thyme, oregano, orange zest, 4 garlic cloves, olive oil, plant-based butter, 1 tsp ground Himalayan pink salt, and ½ tsp ground black pepper, process until minced. Scoop out 1 tbsp of the mixture and set aside.

3. Place the cauliflower florets, thickly sliced carrots, and 4 garlic cloves in the deep roasting pan. Season with ½ tsp ground Himalayan pink salt and ½ tsp ground black pepper and drizzle with olive oil. Place the whole chicken on top of the vegetables, making sure to place the chicken breast side up.

4. Gently loosen the skin of the chicken with your fingers and rub the herb mixture under the skin. Season the outside of the whole chicken with the remaining ground Himalayan pink salt and ground black pepper. Insert the orange quarters, 1 tbsp reserved herb mixture, and the remaining garlic cloves inside the chicken cavity.

5. Roast for 1½ to 2 hours, until fully cooked.

Substitution tip: You can use a lemon in place of the orange.

Per Serving: Calories: 543; Net Carbs: 15g; Protein: 42g; Total Carbs: 21g; Total Fat: 32g

CHICKEN WITH BELL PEPPER THYME SAUCE

COOK TIME: 30 MIN | SERVES: 4

INGREDIENTS:

- 4 (4 oz) chicken breasts, deboned and skinless
- Himalayan pink salt, ground
- Black pepper, ground
- 1 tbsp olive oil
- ½ red onion, finely chopped
- ½ medium red, green, and yellow bell pepper, sliced
- 1 cup chicken broth, low in salt
- 2 tsp thyme, chopped
- ¼ cup coconut cream
- 1 tbsp plant-based butter
- 1 spring onion, chopped

DIRECTIONS:

1. Preheat the oven to 375°F gas mark 5.
2. Season the chicken breasts with ground Himalayan pink salt and ground black pepper.
3. In a large ovenproof frying pan on medium-high heat, add the olive oil and cook until hot.
4. Lightly brown the chicken breasts for 5 minutes on each side. Place the chicken breasts onto a rimmed plate to rest.
5. In the same pan, fry the finely chopped onion until translucent, add the sliced red, green and yellow peppers and fry for 3 minutes until softened.
6. Pour in the chicken broth and chopped thyme. Simmer for 6 minutes until the liquid has reduced by half.
7. Mix in the coconut cream and the plant-based butter and return the chicken breasts and any accumulated juices on the plate into the pan. Allow thickening.
8. Place the ovenproof pan into the oven and bake for 10 minutes until cooked through.
9. Serve hot with the chopped spring onion.

Per Serving: Calories: 287; Net Carbs: 1g; Protein: 34g; Total Carbs: 4g; Total Fat: 14g

ORANGE, GINGER & HONEY LEMON CHICKEN

COOK TIME: 30 MIN | SERVES: 4

INGREDIENTS:

- 4 chicken thighs, deboned and skinless
- 1 tbsp ginger, grated
- Sea salt
- 1 tbsp olive oil
- ½ lemon, juiced and zested
- ½ orange, juiced, and zested
- 2 tbsp honey
- 1 tbsp low-salt soy sauce
- ¼ tsp red pepper flakes
- 1 tbsp parsley, chopped

DIRECTIONS:

1. Season the deboned chicken thighs with ginger and sea salt.

2. Heat the olive oil in a large heavy bottom pan over medium-high heat until hot.

3. Brown the deboned chicken thighs for 5 minutes on each side.

4. In the meantime, while the chicken is browning, mix the lemon juice, lemon zest, orange juice, orange zest, honey, low salt soy sauce, and red pepper flakes in a small bowl.

5. Reduce the heat to low and pour the soy sauce mixture into the pan with the chicken thighs and cover.

6. Simmer for 20 minutes, until the chicken is cooked through, adding some water if necessary.

7. Garnish with chopped parsley and serve.

Ingredient tip: You can serve this with whole wheat rice, wild rice, or vegetables.

Per Serving: Calories: 114; Net Carbs: 9g; Protein: 9g; Total Carbs: 9g; Total Fat: 5g

PESTO PINE NUT, CHICKEN WITH NOODLES

COOK TIME: 10 MIN | SERVES: 4

INGREDIENTS:

- ¼ cup pine nuts, toasted
- 1 tsp garlic, chopped
- ¼ tsp Himalayan pink salt, ground
- 2 cups basil, roughly chopped
- ¼ cup olive oil, plus 1 tablespoon for the noodles
- ¼ cup vegan parmesan cheese, grated and extra for garnish
- 2 medium courgettes, spiraled
- 2 cups chicken breasts, cooked and shredded

DIRECTIONS:

1. For the pesto, add the pine nuts into a heavy bottom pan and lightly toast over medium heat for 3 minutes, until fragrant.

2. Place the toasted pine nuts into a food processor and pulse a few times.

3. Add the chopped garlic and Himalayan pink salt, and process until you have a thick paste.

4. Toss in the roughly chopped basil and process into the pine nuts, adding a ¼ cup of olive oil as it mixes until fully incorporated.

5. Mix in the grated vegan parmesan cheese. Set aside.

6. In a large heavy bottom pan over medium-high, heat the 1 tbsp olive oil until hot.

7. Add the spiraled courgettes and cook, stirring for 1 minute.

8. Toss in the cooked and shredded chicken breasts, and cook for 2 minutes, until hot.

9. Once heated, remove the pan from the heat, and add the homemade basil pesto, and mix gently to coat the courgette noodles and shredded chicken.

10. Garnish with grated vegan parmesan cheese and serve while hot.

Per Serving: Calories: 353; Net Carbs: 3g; Protein: 25g; Total Carbs: 5g; Total Fat: 27g

HERBED CHICKEN & SWEET POTATO BAKE

COOK TIME: 20 MIN | SERVES: 4

INGREDIENTS:

- 2 tbsp coconut oil
- 1 medium onion, sliced
- 2 medium white sweet potatoes, cut into chunks
- 1 lb. cherry tomatoes, halved
- 3 tsp garlic, crushed
- ¼ cup dry white wine
- 4 chicken thighs, deboned and skinless
- 1 tsp mixed herbs
- Sea salt, ground
- Black pepper, ground
- ½ basil, chopped

DIRECTIONS:

1. Preheat the oven to 400°F gas mark 6. Place a deep baking dish to one side.

2. Heat the olive oil in a large heavy bottom pan over medium-high heat until hot.

3. Add the thinly sliced onion, and fry for 2 to 3 minutes, until softened.

4. Add the sweet potato chunks and fry for 1 to 2 minutes, until browned.

5. Mix in the halved cherry tomatoes, crushed garlic, the dry white wine, and mix until incorporated.

6. Season the deboned chicken thighs with mixed herbs, ground sea salt, and ground black pepper.

7. Transfer the vegetable mixture into the deep baking dish and add the chicken thighs onto the vegetables, then place the baking dish into the oven.

8. Roast for 15 minutes, until the chicken thighs are fully cooked and the vegetables are gently browned.

9. Garnish with chopped basil and serve hot.

Per Serving: Calories: 251; Net Carbs: 8g; Protein: 24g; Total Carbs: 11g; Total Fat: 12g

HAM & CHEESE STUFFED CHICKEN BREASTS

COOK TIME: 20 MIN | SERVES: 4

INGREDIENTS:

- 4 chicken breasts, deboned and skinless
- 4 slices cold meats
- 4 slices cheddar cheese
- 1 large egg, beaten
- 1 cup almond flour
- 1 tsp Himalayan pink salt, ground
- 1 tsp black pepper, ground
- 2 tbsp coconut oil

DIRECTIONS:

1. Butterfly the chicken breasts in half horizontally. One side should remain attached.

2. Place 1 slice of cold meat and 1 slice of cheddar cheese on one side of the chicken breasts, close them and secure with wooden toothpicks.

3. In a shallow mixing bowl, add the almond flour, ground Himalayan pink salt and ground black pepper, and mix.

4. Dip the stuffed chicken breasts one at a time into the beaten egg and let it drip, then into the seasoned almond flour.

5. Heat the coconut oil in a large heavy bottom pan over medium-high heat until hot.

6. Gently place in the stuffed chicken breasts, and fry for 8 minutes on each side, until cooked through and the cheese has melted.

Substitution tip: You can use Swiss cheese or blue cheese in place of the cheddar cheese.

Per Serving: Calories: 432; Net Carbs: 4g; Protein: 43g; Total Carbs: 6g; Total Fat: 26g

RICOTTA & TURKEY BELL PEPPERS

COOK TIME: 50 MIN | SERVES: 4

INGREDIENTS:

- Non-stick cooking spray
- 1 tsp olive oil
- 1 lb. turkey breast, ground
- ½ red onion, finely chopped
- 1 tsp garlic, crushed
- 1 tomato, finely chopped
- 2 medium carrots, peeled and cut into small cubes
- ¼ cup peas, thawed
- ½ tsp basil, finely chopped
- Himalayan pink salt
- Black pepper, ground
- 4 medium red bell peppers, tops cut off, seeds removed
- 2 oz ricotta cheese, crumbled
- ¼ cup water

DIRECTIONS:

1. Heat the oven to 350°F or gas mark 4. Use non-stick cooking spray to coat a baking dish and set it aside.

2. In a heavy bottom pan, heat the 1 tsp olive oil until hot.

3. Add the ground turkey into the pan and cook for 6 minutes using a fork to break up the ground turkey until it is browned.

4. Add and fry the finely chopped onion, cubed carrots, thawed peas, and crushed garlic for 3 minutes until softened.

5. Stir in the finely chopped tomato and chopped basil. Season with ground Himalayan pink salt and ground black pepper.

6. Place the red bell peppers cut side up in the baking dish. Spoon the filling equally into the 4 bell pepper.

7. Sprinkle the crumbled ricotta cheese on top of the filling.

8. Gently add ¼ cup of water into the baking dish and cover with aluminum foil.

9. Bake for 40 minutes until the peppers are soft.

Substitution tip: You can use chicken breasts in place of the turkey breasts. You can use feta cheese instead of ricotta cheese.

Per Serving: Calories: 280; Net Carbs: 9g; Protein: 24g; Total Carbs: 14g; Total Fat: 14g

GARLIC & HERB TURKEY PATTIES

COOK TIME: 15 MIN | SERVES: 4

INGREDIENTS:

- 1 lb. lean ground turkey, 93%
- ¼ cup almond flour
- 1 large egg
- 1 onion, finely chopped
- 1 tbsp parsley and thyme, chopped
- ½ tsp garlic, minced
- Himalayan pink salt, ground
- Black pepper, ground
- ¼ tsp coriander, ground
- 4 whole wheat hamburger buns

DIRECTIONS:

1. In a large mixing bowl, combine the ground turkey, almond flour, egg, finely chopped onion, chopped parsley, thyme, minced garlic, ground Himalayan pink salt, ground black pepper, and ground coriander and mix well. Mold the mixture into 4 thin patties.

2. Heat a grill pan on medium-high heat and grill the patties for 6 minutes on each side, until cooked.

3. Place the patties onto the hamburger buns and serve with your choice of toppings.

Optional toppings: spicy barbecue sauce, onion, tomato, lettuce, guacamole, mushrooms, and cheese.

Ingredient tip: You can serve the burgers with sweet potato or butternut fries.

Per Serving (1 burger): Calories: 360; Protein: 39g; Total Carbs: 18g; Total Fat: 21g

ROAST CHICKEN CASSEROLE

COOK TIME: 40 MIN | SERVES: 6

INGREDIENTS:

- ½ cabbage, cut into chunks
- 1 red onion, chopped
- 1 white sweet potato, cut into chunks
- 6 tsp garlic, minced
- 2 tbsp olive oil, divided
- 2 tsp thyme, finely chopped
- Himalayan pink salt, ground
- Black pepper, ground
- 2½ lb. chicken quarters

DIRECTIONS:

1. Preheat the oven to 450°F gas mark 8.

2. Lightly grease a large casserole dish and place the cabbage chunks, chopped onion, sweet potato chunks, and minced garlic in the dish. Add the 1 tbsp of olive oil, sprinkle with the chopped thyme, and season with ground Himalayan pink salt and ground black pepper.

3. Season the chicken to taste.

4. Using a heavy bottom pan on medium heat. Brown the chicken thighs and drumsticks in the remaining 1 tbsp of olive oil, for 10 minutes.

5. Place the browned chicken thighs and drumsticks on top of the vegetables in the casserole dish. Roast the chicken for about 30 minutes.

Per Serving: Calories: 540; Net Carbs: 5g; Protein: 43g; Total Carbs: 14g; Total Fat: 34g

HERB CRUSTED TURKEY BREASTS & VEGGIES

COOK TIME: 2 HOURS | SERVES: 6

INGREDIENTS:

- 2 tsp garlic, minced
- 1 tbsp parsley, finely chopped
- 1 tbsp thyme, finely chopped
- 1 tbsp rosemary, finely chopped
- 2 lb. turkey breasts, deboned and skinless
- 3 tsp avocado oil, divided
- Himalayan pink salt, ground
- Black pepper, ground
- 2 orange sweet potatoes, big cubes
- 2 medium carrots, big cubes
- 2 heads broccoli, cut into florets
- 1 onion, thinly sliced

DIRECTIONS:

1. Heat the oven to 350°F gas mark 4. Cover a large deep roasting pan with aluminum foil. Set it aside.

2. In a small mixing bowl, combine the minced garlic, finely chopped parsley, thyme, and rosemary and mix.

3. Add the deboned turkey breast into the prepared roasting pan and drizzle with 1 tsp avocado oil and rub the herb mixture all over. Season with ground Himalayan pink salt and ground black pepper.

4. Roast the turkey breasts for 30 minutes.

5. Then prepare the sweet potato chunks, carrots chunks, broccoli florets, thinly sliced onion, and mix them together with 2 tsp of avocado oil in a large bowl.

6. Remove the turkey breasts from the oven and place the vegetables around them.

7. Place the turkey breasts with the vegetables back in the oven and roast for 1½ hours until the turkey breasts are cooked and the vegetables are tender.

Per Serving: Calories: 273; Net Carbs: 6g; Protein: 38g; Total Carbs: 20g; Total Fat: 3g

GROUND TURKEY & LENTILS STIR-FRY

COOK TIME: 20 MIN | SERVES: 4

INGREDIENTS:

- 1 tsp olive oil
- 1 lb. lean ground turkey, 93%
- 1 courgette, halved slices
- 1 large red and green bell pepper, sliced
- ½ onion, finely chopped
- 2 tsp garlic, crushed
- 2 tsp oregano, fresh or dried
- 1 cup lentils, cooked
- ¼ cup black olives, pitted and halved
- 1 tbsp balsamic vinegar
- 1 cup spinach, roughly chopped
- Sea salt, ground
- Black pepper, ground

DIRECTIONS:

1. Heat the olive oil in a large heavy bottom pan on medium-high heat until hot.

2. Fry the ground turkey, sliced courgette, sliced red and green bell peppers, finely chopped onion, crushed garlic, and oregano for 10 minutes until the turkey is cooked through and the vegetables are tender.

3. Add the cooked lentils, pitted olives, and balsamic vinegar and cook for 5 minutes until heated through.

4. Remove from the heat, stir in the chopped spinach, and let it sit for 5 minutes until the greens are wilted.

5. Season with ground sea salt and ground black pepper and serve.

Substitution tip: You can use capers in place of olives.

Per Serving (3 cups): Calories: 279; Protein: 27g; Total Carbs: 17g; Total Fat: 12g

SEAFOOD

HAWAIIAN SUSHI TUNA

PREP TIME: 2 HOURS | SERVES: 4

INGREDIENTS:

- 2 lb. fresh tuna, sushi-grade cut into cubes
- 1 cup spring onion, thinly sliced
- 1 cup dark soy sauce
- ¼ cup sesame oil
- 1 tbsp ginger, grated
- Himalayan Pink salt, ground
- Black pepper, ground
- 1 tbsp sesame seeds, lightly toasted

DIRECTIONS:

1. In a medium bowl, add the cubed tuna, sliced spring onion, dark soy sauce, sesame oil, and grated ginger. Season with ground Himalayan pink salt and ground black pepper.

2. Sprinkle over toasted sesame seeds and cover. Place in the fridge for 2 hours or more before serving.

Per Serving: Calories: 375; Net Carbs: 7g; Protein: 50g; Total Carbs: 8g; Total Fat: 16g

TANGY LEMON & LIME SOLE FILLET

COOK TIME: 10 MIN | SERVES: 4

INGREDIENTS:

- 1 tsp chili, powder
- 1 tsp garlic, powder
- ½ tsp lime, zested
- ½ tsp lemon, zested
- ¼ tsp black pepper, ground
- ¼ tsp smoked paprika, ground
- Pinch Himalayan pink salt
- 4 (6 oz) sole fillets, patted dry
- 1 tbsp coconut oil, melted
- 2 tsp lime, juiced

DIRECTIONS:

1. Heat the oven to 450°F gas mark 8.

2. Cover a baking sheet with aluminum foil. Set it aside.

3. In a small mixing bowl, combine the powdered chili, powdered garlic, lime zest, lemon zest, ground black pepper, ground smoked paprika, and Himalayan pink salt, and mix well.

4. Place the patted-dry sole fillets onto the prepared baking sheet and rub the fillets with the spice mixture.

5. Drizzle the melted coconut oil and lime juice onto each sole fillet.

6. Bake for 8 minutes until the fish flakes when pressed lightly with a fork. Serve hot.

Per Serving: Calories: 184; Total Fat: 5g; Total Carbs: 0g; Net Carbs: 0g; Protein: 32g

LIME & SEA BASS CEVICHE

PREP TIME: 4 HOURS | SERVES: 2

INGREDIENTS:

- 1 lb. sushi-grade sea bass, chopped and chilled
- 1½ cups cherry tomatoes, quartered
- 1 cup lime juice
- ¾ cup coriander, finely chopped
- ¼ cup onion, finely chopped
- Sea salt, ground
- Black pepper, ground

DIRECTIONS:

1. In a glass mixing bowl, add the chopped sea bass, quartered cherry tomatoes, lime juice, chopped coriander, and finely chopped onion. Season with ground sea salt and ground black pepper and mix.

2. Marinate the mixture in a fridge for 4 hours or overnight.

3. Serve chilled and enjoy!

Per Serving: Calories: 108; Total Fat: 1g; Protein: 21g; Total Carbs: 4g; Net Carbs: 3g

CAJUN COCONUT CREAM PRAWNS

COOK TIME: 10 MIN | SERVES: 3

INGREDIENTS:

- 2 tsp coconut oil
- ½ red onion, finely chopped
- 1 tbsp Cajun seasoning, shop-bought
- 1 lb. large prawn tails, deshelled and deveined
- ¼ cup coconut cream
- 1 tbsp parsley, finely chopped (optional)

DIRECTIONS:

1. Heat the coconut oil in a large heavy bottom pan over medium-high heat until hot. Fry the finely chopped onion for 3 minutes until soft.

2. Add the Cajun seasoning and fry for 1 minute.

3. Mix in the prawns and fry for 6 minutes until fully cooked and pink, stirring occasionally. Add the coconut cream and stir to incorporate.

4. Garnish with parsley (if using) and serve.

Ingredient tip: If your sauce is too runny, add 2 tbsp of your choice of flour and 4 tbsp of the liquid you are cooking and mix it into a paste. (Add extra liquid into the paste if needed.) Toss it into the mixture and cook until thickened.

Per Serving (about 10 shrimp): Calories: 200; Total Fat: 8g; Total Carbs: 6g; Protein: 31g

SHRIMP & HALIBUT SAUTÉ

COOK TIME: 10 MIN | SERVES: 4

INGREDIENTS:

- 1 lb. large shrimps, deshelled and deveined
- 1 lb. halibut fillet, at room temperature
- Himalayan pink salt, ground
- Black pepper, ground
- 1 tbsp olive oil
- 4 tbsp plant-based butter
- ¼ cup garlic, chopped
- 16 oz baby spinach
- 1 lemon, quartered

DIRECTIONS:

1. Season the shrimp and halibut with ground Himalayan pink salt and ground black pepper.

2. In a heavy bottom pan over medium heat, warm the olive oil. Fry the halibut fillet for 5 minutes, until lightly browned. Add the shrimp and cook for 3 to 5 minutes turning the shrimp and the fillet occasionally, until completely cooked. Remove from the pan and set aside.

3. In the same pan add the plant-based butter and chopped garlic and cook, stirring, for 1 minute. Add the baby spinach and season with ground Himalayan pink salt and ground black pepper and mix until the baby spinach has wilted. Turn off the heat.

4. Distribute the baby spinach evenly between 4 plates and top it with the shrimp and halibut fillet.

5. Serve warm with a lemon quarter on the side for garnish.

Ingredient tip: Seasoning a fish fillet with salt helps to draw out moisture and helps to firm up the fish when you are frying it.

Per Serving: Calories: 382; Total Fat: 18g; Protein: 48g; Total Carbs: 7g; Net Carbs: 4g

FETA & SUN-DRIED TOMATOES PRAWNS

COOK TIME: 30 MIN | SERVES: 4

INGREDIENTS:

- 3 whole tomatoes, chopped
- ½ cup sun-dried tomatoes, chopped
- 2 tsp garlic, crushed
- 2 tsp avocado oil
- 1 tsp oregano, chopped
- Black pepper, ground
- Sea salt, ground
- 1½ lb. (16–20) prawn tails, deshelled and deveined
- 4 tsp lemon juice
- ½ cup ricotta cheese, crumbled

DIRECTIONS:

1. Heat the oven to 450°F gas mark 8.

2. In a medium mixing bowl, add the chopped tomatoes, chopped sun-dried tomatoes, crushed garlic, avocado oil, chopped oregano, and mix until combined. Season with ground black pepper and ground sea salt.

3. Place the tomato mixture in an ovenproof baking dish.

4. Bake for 15 minutes until softened.

5. Mix in the deshelled prawn tails and lemon juice into the hot tomato mixture and top evenly with crumbled ricotta.

6. Bake for a further 15 minutes until the prawns are fully cooked.

Ingredient tip: Soak the sun-dried tomatoes in hot water to soften. The tomatoes will plump up and will be easier to cut and you can use the sun-dried tomato flavored water in your dish.

Per Serving: Calories: 306; Total Fat: 11g; Total Carbs: 12g; Net Carbs: 5g; Protein: 39g

LIME & ORANGE GRILLED SCALLOPS

COOK TIME: 10 MIN | SERVES: 4

INGREDIENTS:

- 2 lb. scallops, cleaned and dried
- Himalayan pink salt
- Black pepper, ground
- 2 tbsp olive oil
- 1 tbsp garlic, minced
- ¼ cup fresh orange juice
- 1 tsp orange zest
- 2 limes, juiced and zested
- 2 tsp thyme, chopped for garnish

DIRECTIONS:

1. Season the clean and dried scallops with ground Himalayan pink salt and ground black pepper.

2. Over medium heat, add the olive oil into a grill pan until hot.

3. Fry the minced garlic for 3 minutes until softened.

4. Gently place the scallops into the pan and cook for 4 minutes on each side, until lightly seared.

5. Place the grilled scallops onto a plate and cover. Set aside.

6. Add the fresh orange juice, orange zest, lime juice, and lime zest into the pan and stir scraping up the bottom bits.

7. Drizzle the orange and lime sauce over the scallops and garnish with chopped thyme and serve.

Per Serving: Calories: 267; Total Fat: 8g; Total Carbs: 8g; Net Carbs: 1g; Protein: 38g

SMOKY MELON SALSA & CRABBY CAKES

COOK TIME: 10 MIN | SERVES: 4

INGREDIENTS:

THE SALSA

- 1 cup honeydew melon, small cubes
- 1 red onion, finely chopped
- 1 medium red bell pepper, small cubes
- 1 tsp thyme, chopped
- Himalayan pink salt, ground
- Smoked paprika, ground
- Black pepper, ground

THE CRAB CAKES

- 1 lb. crab meat, tinned or fresh
- ¼ cup red onion, finely chopped
- ¼ cup breadcrumbs, fine
- 1 tbsp parsley finely chopped
- 1 tsp lemon zest
- 1 egg
- ¼ cup almond flour
- Nonstick cooking spray

DIRECTIONS:

THE SALSA

1. In a small mixing bowl, combine the cubed honeydew melon, finely chopped spring onion, cubed red bell pepper, and chopped thyme.

2. Season the honeydew melon salsa with ground Himalayan pink salt, ground smoked paprika, and ground black pepper. Set aside.

THE CRAB CAKES

3. In a large mixing bowl, add the crab meat, chopped onion, fine breadcrumbs, chopped parsley, lemon zest, and the egg. Mix until well combined.

4. Portion the crab meat mixture into 8 equal portions and mold it into patties.

5. Place the crab cakes into the fridge for 1 hour to firm up.

6. Lightly coat the chilled crab cakes in the almond flour, shaking off any excess flour.

7. Place a large heavy bottom pan over medium heat and lightly coat it with non-stick cooking spray.

8. Fry the crab cakes for 5 minutes on each side until golden brown.

9. Serve warm with the homemade smoky honeydew melon salsa.

Substitution tip: You can use cantaloupe in place of the honeydew melon or try the fruit salsa with chopped peaches.

Per Serving: Calories: 232; Total Fat: 3g; Total Carbs: 18g; Net Carbs: 6g; Protein: 32g

FRIED HADDOCK & CREAMY SUMMER SAUCE

COOK TIME: 10 MIN | SERVES: 4

INGREDIENTS:

- ¼ cup low-fat plain yogurt
- ½ large cucumber, grated and liquid squeezed out
- ½ spring onion, chopped
- 2 tsp mint, finely chopped
- 1 tsp dill, chopped
- 1 tsp honey
- Himalayan Sea salt, ground
- 4 (5 oz) haddock fillets, lightly salted
- Black pepper, ground
- Non-stick cooking spray

DIRECTIONS:

1. In a small bowl, add the low-fat, plain yogurt, grated cucumber, chopped spring onion, chopped mint, chopped dill, honey, and a pinch of ground Himalayan pink salt and mix. Set aside.

2. Dry the haddock fillets with paper towels and season them with ground Himalayan pink salt and ground black pepper.

3. Put a heavy bottom pan on medium-high heat and coat it with non-stick cooking spray.

4. Fry the haddock fillets for 5 minutes on each side, until fully cooked.

5. Transfer haddock fillets onto serving plates.

6. Top with the homemade summer sauce and serve.

Substitution tip: You can use any firm white fish fillets for this recipe.

Per Serving: Calories: 164; Total Fat: 2g; Total Carbs: 4g; Net Carbs: 3g; Protein: 27g

PISTACHIOS & HERB HALIBUT

COOK TIME: 20 MIN | SERVES: 4

INGREDIENTS:

- 4 (5-oz) halibut fillets, lightly salted
- 2 tbsp olive oil, for coating
- ½ cup pistachios, unsalted and finely ground
- 1 tbsp parsley, finely chopped
- 1 tsp thyme, chopped
- 1 tsp basil, finely chopped
- Pinch of Himalayan pink salt, ground
- Black pepper, ground

DIRECTIONS:

1. Warm the oven to 350°F gas mark 4. Cover the baking sheet with aluminum foil, set it aside.

2. Dry the halibut fillets with paper towels and place them on the baking sheet.

3. Coat the dried halibut fillets with olive oil.

4. In a small mixing bowl, add the finely ground pistachios, chopped parsley, chopped thyme, finely chopped basil, ground Himalayan pink salt, and ground black pepper, mix to combine.

5. Spoon the pistachio and herb mixture onto the halibut fish, spreading it out so the tops of the halibut fillets are covered.

6. Bake for 20 minutes until the halibut flakes when pressed with a fork

7. Serve warm.

Substitution tip: Cod would be a great fish to use in this recipe.

Per Serving: Calories: 262; Total Fat: 11g; Total Carbs: 4g; Net Carbs: 1g; Protein: 32g

ZESTY GARLIC SOLE FILLETS

COOK TIME: 20 MIN | SERVES: 4

INGREDIENTS:

- 1 tsp avocado oil
- 4 (5 oz) sole fillets, patted dry
- 3 tbsp plant-based butter
- 2 tsp garlic, crushed
- 2 tbsp almond flour
- 2 cups low-salt chicken broth
- ½ lemon, juiced and zested
- 2 tbsp black olives, pitted and chopped finely

DIRECTIONS:

1. On medium-high heat, add the avocado oil into a large heavy bottom pan until hot.

2. Sear the patted-dry sole fillets for 4 minutes on each side until the fish flakes easily when tested with a fork. Place the cooked fish fillets onto a plate and set it aside.

3. Add the plant-based butter into the same pan.

4. Fry the crushed garlic for 3 minutes until soft.

5. Add the almond flour and whisk until it is a thick paste and cook for 2 minutes stirring.

6. Add the low-salt chicken broth, lemon juice, and lemon zest, and whisk to combine.

7. Cook for 4 minutes stirring constantly until the sauce has thickened.

8. Stir in the finely chopped olives and serve the sauce over the fish.

Substitution tip: You can use capers in place of the olives.

Per Serving: Calories: 271; Total Fat: 13g; Total Carbs: 7g; Net Carbs: 2g; Protein: 30g

ROASTED COD & FRENCH STEW

COOK TIME: 35 MIN | SERVES: 2

INGREDIENTS:

- ½ aubergine, chopped
- 2 courgettes, chopped
- 3 tomatoes, chopped
- 1 red or green bell pepper chopped
- ½ red onion, sliced
- 3 tsp garlic, crushed
- 2 tbsp avocado oil
- 2 tsp oregano, dried
- ¼ tsp cayenne pepper, fresh or ground
- 2 (6oz) cod fillets, lightly salted
- Himalayan pink salt, ground
- Black pepper, ground
- ½ cup feta, crumbled

DIRECTIONS:

1. Warm oven to 400°F gas mark 6. Place aluminum foil on a baking sheet.

2. In a large mixing bowl, add the chopped aubergine, chopped courgettes, chopped tomatoes, chopped red or green bell pepper, sliced red onion, crushed garlic, avocado oil, dried oregano, and fresh or ground cayenne pepper and mix until well combined.

3. Spread the vegetable mixture in the center of the baking sheet and bake for 25 minutes tuning the vegetables halfway.

4. Season the cod fillets with ground Himalayan pink salt and ground black pepper and place the fish fillets on top of the vegetables, baking them for a further 10 minutes.

5. Serve the cod and vegetables hot and topped with crumbled feta.

Substitution tip: You can use crumbled ricotta cheese in place of feta cheese.

Per Serving (1 fillet with 2 cups vegetables): Calories: 286; Total Fat: 13g; Total Carbs: 12g; Protein: 26g

SAUTÉED SPINACH & SALMON

COOK TIME: 30 MIN | SERVES: 4

INGREDIENTS:

- 1 tsp avocado oil
- ½ red onion, finely chopped
- 1 tsp garlic, minced
- 3 cups baby spinach
- 1 cup kale, stems removed and chopped
- Himalayan pink salt, ground
- Black pepper, ground
- 4 (5oz) salmon fillets
- 1 large lemon, quartered

DIRECTIONS:

1. Warm oven to 350°F gas mark 4
2. Heat oil in a heavy bottom pan on medium to high heat.
3. Add garlic and onion into the pan and cook for 3 minutes.
4. Add the spinach and kale and sauté for 5 minutes.
5. Remove heavy bottom pan from the heat and season with Himalayan pink salt and black pepper.
6. Place salmon fillets on top of the greens and bake for 20 minutes.
7. Serve with fresh lemon juice.

Substitution tip: You can use red or green cabbage in place of the kale.

Per Serving: Calories: 281; Total Fat: 16g; Total Carbs: 4g; Net Carbs: 1g; Protein: 29g

STIR-FRIED SUGAR SNAP PEAS & TUNA

COOK TIME: 10 MIN | SERVES: 4

INGREDIENTS:

- 4 (6oz) tuna steaks, patted dry
- 2 tsp olive oil
- Himalayan pink salt, ground
- Black pepper, ground
- 1 tbsp sesame seed oil
- 1 lb. snap peas, trim the ends
- ½ cup turnips, thinly sliced
- 1 tsp ginger, grated
- ¼ cup low-salt soy sauce, low in salt
- 2 tbsp lime juice
- 1 tbsp honey
- Aluminum Foil

DIRECTIONS:

1. Heat heavy bottom pan on medium to high heat.
2. Coat the dried tuna steaks lightly with 1 tsp olive oil and season with ground Himalayan pink salt and ground black pepper
3. Fry tuna steaks in the pan for 2 minutes on each side, remove and rest under foil.
4. Add 1 tsp olive oil and 1 tbsp sesame seed oil to the pan.
5. Add the trimmed snap peas and stir fry for 2 minutes until dark green.
6. Add the sliced turnips and grated ginger and stir fry for 1 minute.
7. Add the low-salt soy sauce, honey, and lime juice and mix it in with the vegetables.
8. Cut tuna into thin slices and serve with the vegetable stir fry on the side.

Per Serving: Calories: 298; Total Fat: 11g; Total Carbs: 13g; Net Carbs: 9g; Protein: 39g

BEEF, PORK & LAMB

SLOW-COOKED ORANGE & PORK SLAW

COOK TIME: 5 HOURS | SERVES: 4

INGREDIENTS:

- 1½ tbsp chili powder, divided
- 2 tbsp ground cumin, divided
- 1½ tsp salt, divided
- 2½ tsp black pepper, divided
- 2 tbsp orange zest, divided
- 3–4 lbs. pork shoulder, fat trimmed
- 6 tsp chopped garlic, divided
- Juice of 2 oranges, divided
- 4 cups green or red cabbage, julienned
- ½ tbsp extra-virgin olive oil

DIRECTIONS:

1. In a small bowl, combine 1 tbsp chili powder, 1 tbsp cumin, 1 tsp salt, 2 tsp black pepper, and 1 tbsp orange zest. Rub the seasoning on the pork shoulder. Set aside.

2. In a slow cooker, add 5 tsp chopped garlic and the juice of 1 orange and mix. Place the seasoned pork shoulder inside, cover, and cook on low for 8 hours or on high for 5 hours. The pork will break apart when cooked properly.

3. Remove the cooked pork shoulder and place it in a dish that will gather the running juices. Shred the meat and place it back into the slow cooker along with the juices. Season to taste.

4. Preheat the oven to broil.

5. On a baking sheet, place the shredded pork and broil for 3 to 4 minutes, until crispy.

6. In a large-sized bowl, add the remaining orange juice, chili powder, cumin, garlic, salt, black pepper, and orange zest. Add the julienned cabbage and olive oil, mix well until well combined.

Substitution tip: Swop the protein for any of your choice.

Tip: If you do not want a citrus flavor, you can add sliced apples in step 2.

Per Serving: Calories: 920; Total Fat: 72g; Protein: 59g; Net Carbs: 5g; Total Carbs: 9g

PICKLED ONION & PORK LETTUCE WRAPS

COOK TIME: 15 MIN | SERVES: 4

INGREDIENTS:

- ½ red onion, thinly sliced
- 2 tbsp red wine vinegar
- Pinch of sea salt
- 1 tbsp olive oil
- 1 tbsp fresh ginger, minced
- 1 tbsp garlic, minced
- ¼ tsp chili flakes
- 1½ lb. ground pork
- 1 red bell pepper, in thin slices
- 1 green bell pepper, in thin slices
- Fresh black pepper
- 4–8 lettuce leaves
- 2 carrots, julienned
- 1 cup cilantro, coarsely chopped

DIRECTIONS:

1. In a small bowl, add the thinly sliced red onion, red wine vinegar, and sea salt and toss to combine.

2. Heat the olive oil in a heavy bottom pan on medium-high heat until hot. Add the minced ginger, garlic, and chili flakes and cook for 30 seconds until fragrant.

3. Add the ground pork and sauté for 7 to 8 minutes, breaking it up with a fork as it cooks. Add the bell pepper slices. Season to taste.

4. Place the lettuce leaves flat on your work surface and divide the pork filling onto each leaf about halfway. Top with the julienned carrots, cilantro, and pickled onion.

5. Roll the lettuce leaves by folding the bottom over the filling and bringing the sides over and roll.

Substitution tip: Replace the lettuce leaves with cabbage leaves by steaming the cabbage for 2 to 3 minutes until al dente.

Per Serving: Calories: 413; Net Carbs: 7g; Protein: 31g; Total Fat: 12g; Total Carbs: 9g

CAULIFLOWER & ROSEMARY COTTAGE PIE

COOK TIME: 20 MIN | SERVES: 4

INGREDIENTS:

- 1 cauliflower head, cored and cut into florets
- 1 tbsp sea salt
- 2 tbsp butter
- 1 tbsp canola oil
- 1 onion, diced
- 2 carrots, cut into small cubes
- 1 celery stalk, diced
- 1 tbsp fresh rosemary, minced
- 1 tsp fresh thyme, minced
- 1 lb. ground beef
- 1 tbsp tomato paste
- ¼ cup red wine
- Salt and pepper

DIRECTIONS:

1. Place the oven rack near the top and preheat the oven to broil.

2. In a large pot, add salt and cauliflower. Fill the pot with enough water to cover the cauliflower and allow to boil and cook for 15 minutes, until tender.

3. Drain the cauliflower and allow most of the liquid to drip and then add it into a food processor. Add the butter and purée until smooth. Set aside.

4. In a heavy bottom pan over medium-high heat, add the canola oil until hot.

5. Add the diced onions, carrots, celery, rosemary, thyme, and salt and cook for 5 minutes until the vegetables begin to soften. Remove from pan.

6. Place the ground beef in the pan and cook for 5 minutes breaking it up with a fork as it cooks and no pink remains.

7. Add the vegetables, tomato paste, and wine and bring to a simmer and cook for a further 2 minutes to allow the alcohol to evaporate. Season to taste.

8. Transfer the meat mixture into an oven-proof dish and spread the cauliflower mash on top. Place under the broiler for 2 to 3 minutes until browned.

Tip: Cook the cauliflower the day before and allow it to drain overnight for most of the liquid to be gone.

Per Serving: Calories: 337; Net Carbs: 11g; Protein: 27g; Total Fat: 17g; Total Carbs: 19g

STEAK & GUACAMOLE TORTILLAS

COOK TIME: 15 MIN | SERVES: 4

INGREDIENTS:

FOR THE GUACAMOLE
- 4 ripe avocados, peeled and pitted
- Pinch of salt
- 1 tsp garlic, minced
- 1 shallot or onion, minced
- 1 tomato chopped, remove the pulp
- ¼ tsp chili flakes (optional)
- 1 tbsp fresh lime juice

FOR THE FILLING
- 3 tbsp olive oil, divided
- 1 tbsp chili powder

- 2 tsp ground coriander
- 2 tsp ground cumin
- 1 tsp salt
- 1 lb. frying steak, thinly sliced
- 1 onion, thinly sliced
- 1 red and green bell pepper, thinly sliced
- 8 lettuce leaves or low-carb tortillas
- 1 cup guacamole

DIRECTIONS:

For the Guacamole:

1. In a medium bowl, mash the ripe avocados with a fork, till slightly lumpy. Add the minced garlic, onion, chopped tomato, chili flakes (optional), and lime juice, mix to combine. Season with salt and pepper. Refrigerate for later.

For the Filling:

2. Combine 2 tbsp of olive oil, chili powder, coriander, cumin, and 1 tsp of salt in a medium bowl and add the thinly sliced steak, toss to coat.

3. Heat a heavy bottom pan over medium-high heat until hot, add the spiced steak slices and fry for 4 minutes. Remove and set aside.

4. Add the remaining 1 tbsp olive oil to the pan and add in the chopped onions and bell peppers, sauté for 5 minutes, until lightly browned. Season to taste.

5. On the lettuce leaves or low-carb tortillas, place the thinly cut steaks and vegetables in the center and top them with homemade guacamole.

Per Serving: Calories: 547; Net Carbs: 10g; Total Fat: 42g; Protein: 28g; Total Carbs: 19g

LAMB & PINE NUT AUBERGINE

COOK TIME: 25 MIN | SERVES: 4

INGREDIENTS:

- 2 medium aubergines, cut into thick slices
- 5 tbsp olive oil, divided
- Sea salt
- Black pepper
- 1 small onion, minced
- 1 lb. ground lamb or pork
- 1 tbsp tomato paste
- 1 tsp garlic, minced
- ⅛ tsp ground allspice
- ½ cup plain yogurt
- ¼ cup pine nuts
- ¼ cup parsley, minced

DIRECTIONS:

1. Preheat the oven to 375°F gas mark 5.

2. In a small heavy bottom pan on medium heat, add the pine nuts and toast until golden and fragrant. Set aside.

3. Toss the aubergine slices in a large bowl with 4 tbsp of olive oil and spread them on a baking sheet. Season with salt and pepper and bake for 25 minutes until lightly browned and soft.

4. In the meantime, in a large pan over medium-high heat, add the remaining 1 tbsp olive oil until hot. Add the onion and cook for 3 minutes until lightly browned.

5. Add the ground lamb or pork, breaking it up with a fork while it cooks for about 5 minutes, and add in the tomato paste. Cook for 2 minutes or until most of the acidity from the paste cooks down.

6. Mix the minced garlic and allspice into the meat mixture and season to taste. Cook for a further minute to incorporate.

7. Arrange the cooked aubergine slices on each plate and top it with the ground lamb or beef mixture. Drizzle with yogurt and sprinkle with toasted pine nuts and parsley.

Substitution tip: To replace the yogurt with a dairy-free option, put a tin of coconut cream in the fridge overnight. When ready to use, skim the cream that has formed on the top and use it in place of the yogurt.

Per Serving: Calories: 625; Net Carbs: 9g; Protein: 24g; Total Fat: 60g; Total Carbs: 20g

GARLIC YOGURT & LAMB LETTUCE CUPS

COOK TIME: 15 MIN | SERVES: 4

INGREDIENTS:

- 1 lb. ground lamb
- 1 tbsp garlic, chopped and divided
- ½ tbsp oregano, finely chopped
- 1 lemon, juiced and divided
- 3 tsp olive oil, divided
- ¾ tsp sea salt, ground
- ¾ tsp black pepper, ground
- ½ cup low-fat yogurt, plain
- 8 crisp lettuce leaves
- 2 cups romaine lettuce, shredded
- ½ cup ricotta cheese, crumbled

DIRECTIONS:

1. In a large mixing bowl, add the ground lamb, ½ tbsp of chopped garlic, chopped oregano, half of the lemon juice, 2 tsp of olive oil, ground sea salt, and ground black pepper and mix.

2. Add the remaining olive oil into a heavy bottom pan on medium-high heat until hot.

3. Add in the ground lamb mixture and cook for 8 minutes until browned. Remove from the heat.

4. In a small mixing bowl, combine the plain yogurt and the remaining chopped garlic and lemon juice, and season with ground sea salt and ground black pepper.

5. Place 2 crisp lettuce leaves onto each plate and assemble the lettuce cup in this order: ground lamb, shredded lettuce, crumbled ricotta cheese, yogurt, and garlic sauce.

Per Serving: Calories: 463; Total Fat: 35g; Protein: 31g; Total Carbs: 6g; Net Carbs: 5g

GRILLED RIBEYE WITH MUSHROOMS & ONIONS

COOK TIME: 25 MIN | SERVES: 4

INGREDIENTS:

- 4 (5 oz) rib-eye steaks, room temperature
- Sea salt, ground
- Black pepper, ground
- 2 tbsp olive oil, divided
- 4 tbsp plant-based butter
- 3 tsp garlic, crushed
- 4 cups button mushrooms, sliced
- 1 medium red onion, thinly sliced
- 1 tbsp Worcestershire sauce

DIRECTIONS:

1. Dry the steaks with paper towels and season with ground sea salt and ground black pepper.

2. Heat 1 tbsp of olive oil in a large grill pan over medium-high heat, until hot. Add the steaks and cook for 2 minutes on each side, until browned.

3. Bring the temperature to medium heat and add the plant-based butter, letting it melt completely. Spoon the melted plant-based butter over the steaks until cooked to your preference. Place the cooked steaks onto a platter and pour the butter over them. Rest for 10 minutes.

4. In the same pan over medium-high heat, add the remaining 1 tbsp of olive oil and the crushed garlic and cook until fragrant. Add the sliced mushrooms and sliced onions and cook for about 8 minutes, until tender and browned. Add the Worcestershire sauce and cook for 2 minutes. Season with ground sea salt and ground black pepper.

5. Serve the steaks with fried mushrooms and onions.

Per Serving: Calories: 579; Total Fat: 49g; Protein: 28g; Total Carbs: 6g; Net Carbs: 5g

MUSHROOM PEPPERCORN FILET MIGNON

COOK TIME: 25 MIN | SERVES: 4

INGREDIENTS:

- 4 (5 oz) filet mignon steaks, room temperature
- Sea salt, ground
- Black pepper, ground
- 2 tbsp avocado oil, divided
- 1 lb. portobello mushrooms, sliced
- ½ medium yellow onion, sliced
- 3 tsp garlic, finely chopped
- 4 tbsp plant-based butter
- 6 sage leaves, finely chopped

DIRECTIONS:

1. Pat the filet mignon steaks dry with paper towels. Season with ground sea salt and ground black pepper.

2. In a large heavy bottom pan over medium-high heat, add 1 tbsp of avocado oil until hot. Add the steaks and cook on both sides until they are to your liking. Place the steaks onto a plate and set them aside.

3. Bring the heat down to medium and add the remaining 1 tbsp of avocado oil. Add the sliced mushrooms and sliced onions and cook for 5 to 7 minutes. Add the chopped garlic and cook for 2 minutes. Season with ground sea salt and ground black pepper and add it to the plate with the steaks.

4. Add the plant-based butter and chopped sage leaves to the pan and cook for 3 to 5 minutes, until the butter has melted and browned. Discard the sage leaves.

5. Top the steaks with the fried mushrooms and fried onions and drizzle them with the sage brown butter and serve.

Per Serving: Calories: 420; Total Fat: 28g; Protein: 36g; Total Carbs: 6g; Net Carbs: 4g

SHERRY ROASTED BEEF & PEPPER SAUCE

COOK TIME: 1 HOUR 40 MIN | SERVES: 4

INGREDIENTS:

- 1½ lb. rump beef roast
- Himalayan pink salt, fine
- Black pepper, ground
- 3 tsp olive oil, divided
- 3 small onions, minced
- 2 tsp garlic, minced
- 1 tbsp green peppercorns
- 2 tbsp sherry
- 2 tbsp almond flour
- 1 cup beef broth, no salt

DIRECTIONS:

1. Heat the oven to 300°F gas mark 2.

2. Generously season the beef roast with fine Himalayan pink salt and ground black pepper.

3. In a cast-iron pan over medium-high heat add 2 tsp of olive oil and cook until hot.

4. Brown the beef on all sides, about 10 minutes in total, and place it into a baking dish.

5. Roast the beef until cooked to your satisfaction, about 1½ hours for medium cooked. When the roast has been in the oven for 1 hour, start the pepper sauce.

6. In the same pan over medium-high heat, fry the minced onion in the remaining 1 tsp of olive oil for 4 minutes until soft.

7. Stir in the minced garlic and green peppercorns and cook for 1 minute. Whisk in the sherry to deglaze the pan.

8. Whisk in the almond flour to form a thick paste, cook for 1 minute stirring constantly.

9. Add the no-salt beef broth and whisk for 4 minutes until the sauce is thick and glossy. Season the sauce with fine Himalayan pink salt and ground black pepper.

10. Carve and serve the beef with a generous spoonful of sauce.

Per Serving: Calories: 330; Total Fat: 18g; Total Carbs: 4g; Net Carbs: 1g; Protein: 36g

BASIL MEATBALL BAKE

COOK TIME: 15 MIN | SERVES: 4

INGREDIENTS:

- Non-stick cooking spray
- ½ lb. ground pork, lean
- ½ lb. ground beef, lean
- 1 onion, finely chopped
- ¼ cup breadcrumbs
- 2 tbsp basil, chopped
- 2 tsp garlic, minced
- 1 egg
- Pinch Himalayan pink salt, ground
- Pinch black pepper, ground
- Marinara sauce
- Vegetable of your choice

DIRECTIONS:

1. Heat the oven to 350°F gas mark 4.

2. Coat a baking tray with non-stick cooking spray and set it aside.

3. In a large mixing bowl, add the ground pork, ground beef, chopped onion, breadcrumbs, chopped basil, minced garlic, egg, ground Himalayan pink salt, and ground black pepper and mix well to combine.

4. Roll the ground meat into medium-sized meatballs.

5. Put the meatballs onto the baking tray and bake for 15 minutes until browned and cooked through.

6. Serve the meatballs with marinara sauce and some steamed green beans or any vegetable of your choice.

Ingredient tip: You can serve this with spaghetti squash or courgette noodles.

Per Serving: Calories: 332; Net Carbs: 3g; Protein: 24g; Total Carbs: 13g; Total Fat: 19g

ROAST PORK TENDERLOIN WITH APPLE SLAW

COOK TIME: 20 MIN | SERVES: 4

INGREDIENTS:

- 2 tbsp avocado oil, divided
- 1 (1¼ lb.) pork tenderloin, boneless and patted dry
- Himalayan pink salt, ground
- Black pepper, ground
- 1 tbsp rosemary, chopped
- 1 Granny Smith apple, cored, seeded cut into wedges
- ½ red cabbage, thinly sliced and core removed
- ½ red onion, thinly sliced
- 1 tbsp apple cider vinegar
- ½ cup parsley, roughly chopped
- 1 tbsp mint, chopped

DIRECTIONS:

1. Preheat the oven to 425°F gas mark 7.
2. Heat 1 tbsp avocado oil in a large cast-iron pan over medium heat until hot.
3. Rub the dried pork generously with ground Himalayan pink salt, ground black pepper, and the finely chopped rosemary.
4. Transfer the pork into the pan, and sear for about 10 minutes, until browned on all sides.
5. In a large mixing bowl, add the apple wedges, sliced cabbage, and sliced onion with the remaining 1 tbsp of avocado oil. Scatter the mixture around the pork in the cast iron pan.
6. Place the pan into the oven, and roast for 10 minutes, until the pork is fully cooked, and the vegetables are tender.
7. Put the cooked pork onto a cutting board and allow to rest.
8. Add the apple cider vinegar, chopped mint, and chopped parsley into the pan with the apple wedges and cabbage and mix well.
9. Slice the pork and serve with the slaw.

Per Serving: Calories: 263; Net Carbs: 10g; Protein: 28g; Total Carbs: 15g; Total Fat: 11g

BEEF & MUSHROOM CASSEROLE

COOK TIME: 15 MIN | SERVES: 4

INGREDIENTS:

- 1 tbsp olive oil
- 1 lb. rib eye steak, thinly sliced
- 1 onion, thinly sliced
- 8 oz mushrooms, sliced
- ¼ cup brandy or dry white wine
- ¾ cup beef stock
- 1 tsp whole-grain mustard
- ½ cup sour cream
- Himalayan pink salt, ground
- Black pepper, ground
- ¼ cup parsley, roughly chopped

DIRECTIONS:

1. Heat the olive oil in a large heavy bottom pan over high heat until hot.

2. Add the steak and fry for 2 to 3 minutes on each side, until semi-cooked through. Place into a dish.

3. Cook the sliced onion and sliced mushrooms for 5 minutes, until tender.

4. Carefully add the brandy or white wine to deglaze the pan, scraping up the browned bits from the bottom. Cook for 1 minute for the alcohol to evaporate.

5. Add the beef stock and whole-grain mustard and bring to a simmer, cook for 2 to 3 minutes, until reduced.

6. Return the beef to the pan and cook for 2 to 3 minutes.

7. Remove the pan from the heat and stir in the sour cream. Season with ground Himalayan pink salt and ground black pepper.

8. Place the cooked beef and mushrooms onto a serving dish, and sprinkle with the chopped parsley.

Ingredient tip: To replace the sour cream, you can use ½ cup dairy-free cottage cheese and 2 tsp lemon juice and mix them together. .

Per Serving: Calories: 328; Net Carbs: 6g; Protein: 28g; Total Carbs: 8g; Total Fat: 20g

FRUITY BACON & VEG BAKE

COOK TIME: 15 MIN | SERVES: 4

INGREDIENTS:

- Non-stick cooking spray
- 6 cups brussels sprouts, halved
- ¼ lb. bacon, chopped
- 1 onion, sliced
- ½ red apple, peeled, cored, and chopped
- 4 tsp garlic, chopped
- 2 tbsp olive oil, divided
- 2½ tsp sea salt, ground and divided
- 1½ tsp black pepper, ground and divided
- 2–2½ lb. pork tenderloin

DIRECTIONS:

1. Preheat the oven to 425°F gas mark 7. Coat a roasting pan with non-stick cooking spray.

2. In a large mixing bowl, combine the brussels sprout halves, chopped bacon, sliced onion, chopped apple, chopped garlic, and 1 tbsp of olive oil and mix. Add the ½ tsp of ground sea salt and ½ tsp of ground black pepper and mix.

3. Rub the pork tenderloin with the remaining ground sea salt, ground black pepper, and olive oil. Place it in the center of the roasting pan. Spread the fruit and veg mixture around the pork.

4. Bake for 30 minutes, until the pork is fully cooked.

5. Serve hot.

Substitution tip: You can add any vegetables you want into this dish.

Per Serving: Calories: 544; Net Carbs: 12g; Protein: 63g; Total Carbs: 19g; Total Fat: 24g

LIME LAMB CHOPS

COOK TIME: 10 MIN | SERVES: 4

INGREDIENTS:

- ¼ cup olive oil
- ¼ cup lime juice
- 2 tbsp lime zest
- 2 tbsp mint, chopped
- 2 tbsp parsley, chopped
- Pinch of Himalayan pink salt, ground
- Pinch black pepper, ground
- 12 lamb chops

DIRECTIONS:

1. In a small mixing bowl, whisk together the olive oil, lime juice, lime zest, chopped parsley, chopped mint, ground Himalayan pink salt, and ground black pepper.

2. Transfer the mixture into a marinading dish with a lid.

3. Add the lamb chops into the marinading dish and cover with the lid. Mix to combine.

4. Place the dish with the marinated lamb for 4 hours in the fridge, turning several times.

5. Preheat the oven to broil.

6. Remove the chops from the dish and arrange them on an aluminum foil-lined baking sheet. Discard the remaining marinade.

7. Broil the lamb chops for 4 minutes on each side.

8. Rest the lamb chops for 5 minutes before serving.

Ingredient tip: Mint goes perfectly with lamb. You can cook down the remaining marinade and thicken it into a sauce for the lamb chops.

Per Serving: Calories: 413; Net Carbs: 0g; Protein: 31g; Total Carbs: 1g; Total Fat: 29g

SPICY LAMB CASSEROLE

COOK TIME: 2 HOUR 15 MINS | SERVES: 4

INGREDIENTS:

- 2 tbsp canola oil
- 1½ lb. organic lamb shoulder, cut into chunks
- ½ sweet onion, finely chopped
- 1 tbsp ginger, grated
- 2 tsp garlic, minced
- 1 tsp cinnamon, ground
- 1 tsp cumin, ground
- ¼ tsp cloves, ground
- 2 white sweet potatoes, peeled and diced
- 2 cups beef broth, low sodium
- Himalayan pink salt, fine
- Black pepper, ground
- 2 tsp parsley, chopped for garnish
- 2 tsp mint, finely chopped

DIRECTIONS:

1. Heat the oven to 300°F gas mark 2.

2. Place a large heavy bottom pan over medium-high heat and add the canola oil.

3. Add the lamb chunks and fry for 6 minutes until browned, stirring occasionally.

4. Add the chopped onion, grated ginger, minced garlic, ground cinnamon, ground cumin, and ground cloves, and fry for 5 minutes.

5. Add the diced sweet potatoes and low sodium beef broth and bring the stew to a boil.

6. Transfer the lamb mixture into an ovenproof casserole dish and cover with a lid or aluminum foil and place into the oven. Cook for 2 hours, stirring occasionally until the lamb is tender.

7. Remove the stew from the oven and season with fine Himalayan pink salt and ground black pepper.

8. Garnish with chopped parsley and mint and serve hot.

Ingredient tip: mint pairs perfectly with most lamb dishes. Mint also helps to relieve indigestion.

Per Serving Calories: 545; Total Fat: 35g; Total Carbs: 16g; Net Carbs: 4g; Protein: 32g

SOUPS & STEWS

AVO & CUCUMBER SOUP

PREP TIME: 10 MIN | SERVES: 4

INGREDIENTS:

- 2 ripe avocados, peeled and pip removed
- 2 cucumbers, skinned and seeds removed
- 1 (13.5 oz) coconut milk, canned
- 1 tbsp lime juice
- 2 tsp rice vinegar
- 1 tsp chili paste
- Himalayan pink salt, ground
- 1 tbsp olive oil
- ½ cup basil, chopped
- 1 tbsp chives, chopped

DIRECTIONS:

1. Add the peeled avocado, skinned cucumber, coconut milk, lime juice, rice vinegar, chili paste, and ground Himalayan pink salt into a blender and purée until smooth. Add 1 tbsp of water at a time to thin the mixture to the consistency of pancake batter.

2. Place the soup in the fridge for 30 minutes to 3 hours.

3. Drizzle with olive oil and sprinkle the chopped basil and chives. Serve cold.

Per Serving: Calories: 426; Net Carbs: 0g; Protein: 5g; Total Carbs: 20g; Total Fat: 40g

KALE & CAULIFLOWER SOUP

COOK TIME: 30 MIN | SERVES: 4

INGREDIENTS:

- 2 tbsp avocado oil
- 8 oz green beans, cut into pieces
- 10 oz cauliflower, florets
- 1 tbsp garlic, minced
- 8 cups vegetable stock
- 1 can tomatoes, diced
- 2 cups kale, chopped
- Sea salt, ground
- Black pepper, ground
- 1 tbsp parsley, chopped (optional
- 1 tbsp coriander, chopped (optional)
- 1 tbsp chives, chopped (optional)
- ½ lemon, juice (optional)

DIRECTIONS:

1. Heat the avocado oil in a large pot over medium heat. Add the cut green beans pieces and cauliflower florets and cook for 7 to 9 minutes, stirring occasionally, until lightly brown. Add the minced garlic and cook for 2 minutes, stirring occasionally.

2. Increase the heat to high, and add the vegetable stock, diced tomatoes, and chopped kale, and bring to a boil. Reduce the heat to low, let simmer gently for 15 to 20 minutes, until the vegetables are tender.

3. Season with ground sea salt and ground black pepper. Serve with a sprinkle of fresh parsley, coriander, chives and lemon juice (if using) for extra flavor.

Per Serving: Calories: 222; Net Carbs: 13g; Protein: 14g; Total Carbs: 19g; Total Fat: 10g

CREAM OF CHICKEN & MUSHROOM SOUP

COOK TIME: 15 MIN | SERVES 4

INGREDIENTS:

- 2 tbsp coconut oil
- 1½ lb. chicken breast, cubed
- 1 onion, finely diced
- 2 cups mushrooms, sliced
- ½ tbsp garlic, minced
- 4 cups chicken stock
- 1 cup milk, low fat
- 1 cup heavy cream
- Sea salt, ground
- Black pepper, ground
- 2 tbsp parsley, finely chopped(optional)

DIRECTIONS:

1. In a pot over medium heat, warm the olive oil and add the cubed chicken, diced onion, sliced mushrooms, and minced garlic cook stirring until the chicken begins to brown.

2. Add the chicken stock, low-fat milk, and heavy cream, and reduce to a simmer on low for 10 minutes until the chicken is cooked through. Sprinkle with chopped parsley, ground sea salt, and ground black pepper to taste.

Ingredient tip: Adding the chopped parsley adds a completely different taste to the chicken soup.

Per Serving: Calories: 473; Net Carbs: 9g; Protein: 46g; Total Carbs: 12g; Total Fat: 27g

CREAMY LOW-CARB RED PEPPER SOUP

COOK TIME: 40 MIN | SERVES: 4

INGREDIENTS:

- 4 red bell peppers
- 7 tsp garlic, chopped
- 2 tbsp avocado oil, extra for drizzling
- ½ cup onion, finely chopped
- 4 cups vegetable or chicken stock
- 3 tbsp tomato paste
- ½ cup whipping cream
- Sea salt, ground
- Black pepper, ground

DIRECTIONS:

1. Preheat the oven to 400°F gas mark 6 and line a baking sheet with aluminum foil.

2. Place the red bell peppers and garlic on the lined baking sheet and coat with avocado oil.

3. Roast for 30 minutes, turning the peppers and garlic every 10 minutes to prevent burning.

4. Remove the garlic and set it aside. Remove the skin, seeds, and stems from the bell peppers and place the bell peppers into a bowl, and set aside.

5. In a medium pot over medium heat, add the 2 tbsp of avocado oil. Add the chopped onions and cook for 7 minutes, stirring, until brown.

6. Purée the vegetable or chicken stock, tomato paste, chopped onions, garlic, and roasted peppers in a blender until smooth. Pour the bell pepper mixture into the pot and add the whipping cream.

7. Season with ground sea salt and ground black pepper. Simmer for 10 minutes, until hot.

Per Serving: Calories: 243; Net Carbs: 12g; Protein: 3g; Total Carbs: 15g; Total Fat: 19g

TURKEY & SWEET POTATO SOUP

COOK TIME: 30 MIN | SERVES 4

INGREDIENTS:

- 1 tbsp olive oil
- 1 onion, chopped
- 2 celery stalks, chopped
- 2 tsp garlic, minced
- 4 cups cabbage, julienned
- 1 white sweet potato, skin removed and diced
- 8 cups chicken stock
- 2 bay leaves
- 1 cup turkey breast, cooked and chopped
- 2 tsp thyme, chopped
- Himalayan pink salt, ground
- Black pepper, ground

DIRECTIONS:

1. In a large pot add the olive oil over medium heat.
2. Fry the chopped onion, chopped celery stalks, and minced garlic for 3 minutes until softened.
3. Add the julienned cabbage and diced sweet potato and fry for 3 minutes.
4. Pour in the chicken stock and add the bay leaves and bring to a boil.
5. Reduce the heat to low and simmer for 20 minutes until the vegetables are tender.
6. Add the cooked turkey and chopped thyme and simmer for 4 minutes until the turkey is heated through.
7. Remove the bay leaves and season the soup with ground Himalayan pink salt and ground black pepper.

Substitution tip: You can use chicken breasts in place of the turkey breasts.

Per Serving: Calories: 325; Net Carbs: 13g; Protein: 24g; Total Carbs: 30g; Total Fat: 11g

QUINOA & BEEF SOUP

COOK TIME: 30 MIN | SERVES: 4

INGREDIENTS:

- 2 tsp olive oil
- 1 small red onion, chopped
- 1 tbsp garlic, crushed
- 4 celery stalks, with greens and chopped
- 2 medium carrots, diced and peeled
- 1 white sweet potato, diced and peeled
- 8 cups low-salt beef broth
- 1 cup quinoa, cooked
- 2 cups beef cubes, cooked and cut
- 2 bay leaves
- 2 tsp sriracha sauce
- 2 tsp thyme, chopped
- 1 cup kale, julienned
- Himalayan pink salt, ground
- Black pepper, ground

DIRECTIONS:

1. Place a large deep pot over medium-high heat and add the olive oil.
2. Fry the chopped onion and crushed garlic for 3 minutes until softened.
3. Add the chopped celery, diced carrot, and diced sweet potato, and cook for 5 minutes stirring occasionally.
4. Gently add the low-salt beef broth, cooked quinoa, beef cubes, bay leaves, and sriracha sauce.
5. Once the soup is boiling, reduce the heat to low.
6. Simmer gently for 15 minutes until the vegetables are tender.
7. Discard the bay leaves and mix in the chopped thyme and julienned kale.
8. Continue to cook for 5 minutes and season with ground Himalayan pink salt and ground black pepper.

Substitute tip: You can use farro, oats, or brown rice in place of the quinoa.

Per Serving: Calories: 345; Total Fat: 11g; Total Carbs: 33g; Net Carbs: 8g; Protein: 28g

ROAST VEGGIES & GOAT CHEESE SOUP

COOK TIME: 35 MIN | SERVES: 6

INGREDIENTS:

- 2 tbsp avocado oil, plus extra
- 16 Roma tomatoes, halved
- 4 medium red bell peppers, halved and seeds removed
- 4 celery stalks, roughly chopped
- 1 red onion, cut into eight
- 6 tsp garlic, crushed
- Himalayan pink salt, ground
- Black pepper, ground
- 6 cups chicken broth, low in salt
- 2 tbsp basil, chopped
- 2 oz goat cheese, crumbled

DIRECTIONS:

1. Preheat the oven to 400°F gas mark 6.

2. Lightly coat a large baking dish with avocado oil.

3. Add the halved tomatoes cut side down onto the oiled dish. Scatter the halved red bell peppers, chopped celery, cut onion, and crushed garlic onto the tomatoes.

4. Add 2 tbsp of avocado oil onto the vegetables and season with ground Himalayan pink salt and ground black pepper. Mix to combine.

5. Roast the vegetables for 30 minutes until soft and slightly charred. Remove from oven.

6. In a food processor or blender, purée the vegetables with the chicken broth in batches until smooth.

7. Transfer the vegetable and broth puréed soup into a medium-sized pot over medium-high heat and bring the soup to a simmer.

8. Mix in the chopped basil and crumbled goat cheese just before serving.

Substitute tip: You can use cream cheese in place of the goat cheese. You can add plain yogurt in small amounts into the cream cheese to add that tangy flavor.

Per Serving: Calories: 188; Total Fat: 10g; Total Carbs: 21g; Net Carbs: 14g; Protein: 8g

CARROT & LENTIL SOUP

COOK TIME: 55 MIN | SERVES: 8

INGREDIENTS:

- 1 tsp olive oil
- 1 medium onion, chopped
- 1 tbsp garlic, minced
- 4 celery stalks, with the greens, chopped
- 1 quartered white cabbage, roughly chopped
- 3 medium carrots, diced and peeled
- 3 cups red or brown lentils, picked over, washed, and drained
- 4 cups low-salt vegetable broth
- 3 cups water
- 2 bay leaves
- 2 tsp thyme, chopped
- Sea salt, ground
- Black pepper, ground

DIRECTIONS:

1. Heat the olive oil in a large cooking pot on medium-high heat until hot.

2. Fry the chopped onion and minced garlic for 3 minutes until translucent.

3. Add the chopped celery with the greens and diced carrots, mix and fry for 5 minutes.

4. Stir in the red or brown lentils, vegetable broth, water, and bay leaves, and bring the soup to a boil.

5. Reduce the heat to low and simmer gently for 45 minutes until the lentils are soft and the soup is thick.

6. Discard the bay leaves and stir in the thyme.

7. Season with ground sea salt and ground black pepper and serve hot.

Ingredient tip: when cooking with lentils, "picked over" means that you need to rid the lentils of any debris and stones.

Per Serving: Calories: 284; Total Fat: 2g; Total Carbs: 47g; Net Carbs: 4g; Protein: 20g

CREAM OF BUTTERNUT SOUP

COOK TIME: 25 MIN | SERVES: 4

INGREDIENTS:

- 1 tbsp coconut oil
- 1 medium onion, finely chopped
- 1 tsp garlic, minced
- 1 tsp ginger, peeled and grated, or 1 teaspoon ground
- 6 cups low-salt vegetable broth
- 1 small butternut, peeled, seeded, and cut into chunks
- 2 tsp cumin, ground
- ½ tsp coriander, ground
- ½ cup coconut cream
- Sea salt, ground
- Black pepper, ground
- ¼ cup pumpkin seeds, toasted
- 2 tbsp cilantro, chopped

DIRECTIONS:

1. In a large stockpot, heat the coconut oil over medium-high heat. Fry the chopped onion, minced garlic, and grated ginger for 4 minutes until softened.

2. Pour in the vegetable broth, butternut chunks, ground cumin, and ground coriander, and bring to a boil. Reduce the heat to low and simmer for 20 minutes until the vegetables are tender.

3. Using an immersion blender or a stand blender, purée the vegetables until smooth, being careful with splatter. Add the coconut cream and season with ground sea salt and ground black pepper and whisk.

4. Serve in bowls and top with the toasted pumpkin seeds and chopped cilantro.

Time Saver: When you make butternut, keep the seeds and toast them yourself for future recipes needing toasted pumpkin seeds. Toss the pumpkin seeds with a bit of olive oil and roast them on a baking sheet for 45 minutes in a 400°F oven.

Ingredient tip: adding the zest of 1 orange into the butternut soup is a perfect winter warmer and is packed with Vitamin C.

Per Serving (2 cups): Calories: 237; Total Carbs: 29g; Total Fat: 14g; Protein: 4g

ITALIAN FISH STEW

COOK TIME: 20 MIN | SERVES: 4

INGREDIENTS:

- 3 tbsp olive oil
- 1 brown onion, diced
- 3 tbsp garlic, minced
- ½ cup plum tomatoes, roughly chopped
- ¼ tsp red pepper flakes
- 2 tbsp tomato paste
- ½ cup white wine
- 8 cups vegetable broth or seafood stock
- 1½ lb. clams or mussels, scrubbed and debearded
- 1 lb. cod fillets, cut into pieces
- ½ lb. large shrimp, peeled and deveined
- Sea salt, ground
- Black pepper, ground

- 2 scallions, thinly sliced
- ½ bunch parsley, finely chopped
- ½ lemon, juiced

DIRECTIONS:

1. Heat the olive oil in a large stockpot over medium-high heat until hot.

2. Add the diced onion, and cook for 5 minutes, until softened.

3. Add the minced garlic, chopped tomatoes, and red pepper flakes, and cook for 2 minutes, until fragrant.

4. Add the tomato paste, and cook for 2 minutes, until caramelized.

5. Pour in the white wine and vegetable or seafood broth and bring it to a simmer.

6. Add the clean clams or mussels and cook for 5 minutes covered with a lid.

7. Add the cod fillets and replace the lid and cook for 2 minutes.

8. Mix in the peeled shrimp and replace the lid and cook for 3 minutes. The mussels should all be open by then. The mussels that are not open after 10 minutes should be discarded. Season with ground sea salt and ground black pepper.

9. Mix in the chopped scallions, chopped parsley, and lemon juice just before serving.

Substitution tip: you can use any firm, white fish like halibut in this recipe.

Per Serving: Calories: 479; Total Fat: 18g; Total Carbs: 17g; Net Carbs: 13g; Protein: 57g

CREAMY INDIAN CHICKEN CURRY

COOK TIME: 35 MIN | SERVES: 4

INGREDIENTS:

- 2 tsp organic butter
- 3 (5 oz) chicken breasts, boneless, skinless, and cubed
- 1 tbsp ginger, grated
- 1 tbsp garlic, crushed
- 2 tbsp mild or hot curry powder or paste
- 2 cups low-salt chicken broth
- 1 cup coconut cream, canned
- ¼ cup raisins (optional)
- 1 carrot, peeled and diced
- 1 white sweet potato, peeled and diced
- 2 tbsp cilantro, chopped

DIRECTIONS:

1. Place a medium-sized stockpot over medium-high heat and add the organic butter.

2. Fry the cubed chicken breasts for 10 minutes until lightly browned and slightly cooked.

3. Add the grated ginger, crushed garlic, and curry powder, and fry for 3 minutes until fragrant.

4. Add the low sodium chicken broth, coconut cream, raisins (if using), diced carrot, and diced sweet potato, and bring it to a boil.

5. Lower the heat and let it simmer for 20 minutes, stirring occasionally until the vegetables and chicken is tender.

6. Mix in the chopped cilantro and serve.

Ingredient tip: You can serve this with brown rice, wild rice, basmati rice, or gluten-free naan bread. Adding the raisins will give you a sweet and spicy flavor.

Substitution tip: If you do not want to use coconut cream, you can replace it with a dairy-free, heavy cream alternative.

Per Serving: Calories: 327; Total Fat: 17g; Total Carbs: 15g; Net Carbs: 4g; Protein: 29g

ZUCCHINI & TOMATO STEW

COOK TIME: 20 MIN | SERVES: 4 – 6

INGREDIENTS:

- 1 tbsp plant-based butter
- 2 medium white onions, diced
- 3 cups (12 oz) zucchini, trimmed and sliced
- 2½ cups medium tomatoes, cored and chopped
- 1 tsp Cajun seasoning

DIRECTIONS:

1. In a large cast-iron pan, melt the plant-based butter over medium heat.

2. Add the diced onion and fry until translucent and lightly browned.

3. Add the sliced zucchini and fry for 5 minutes, until browned.

4. Mix in the chopped tomatoes and Cajun seasoning and cook for 10 minutes until the zucchini is tender and the tomatoes have broken down.

Per Serving: Calories: 87; Total Fat: 3g; Total Carbs: 13g; Protein: 3g

CHOCOCHILI CON CARNE

COOK TIME: 20 MIN | SERVES: 4

INGREDIENTS:

- 1 lb. beef or turkey, ground
- 1 tbsp garlic, minced
- 1 (28 oz) can diced tomatoes
- 2 tbsp chili powder
- 1½ tbsp cumin, ground
- 2–3 oz unsweetened chocolate, dark
- Sea salt, fine
- Black pepper, ground

DIRECTIONS:

1. In a large stockpot over medium-high heat, add the ground beef or turkey and cook for 10 minutes breaking it up with a fork, until browned. Drain any excess grease.

2. Fry the minced garlic for 2 minutes. Reduce the heat to low and add the diced tomatoes, chili powder, ground cumin, and dark chocolate. Let it simmer, covered for 10 minutes.

3. Season with fine sea salt and ground black pepper and serve.

Ingredient tip: You can also use the chili-flavored dark chocolate.

Per Serving: Calories: 366; Total Fat: 22g; Protein: 25g; Total Carbs: 17g; Net Carbs: 9g

VEGETARIAN

CHIPOTLE CASHEW NOODLES

PREP TIME: 10 MIN | SERVES: 4

INGREDIENTS:

- 2 medium summer squash
- ½ cup raw unsalted cashews, soaked in fresh water overnight
- ½ cup water
- 1–2 tsp chipotle peppers, minced in adobo sauce
- 1 lime, juiced
- ½ tsp sea salt, fine
- 1 large ripe avocado, pitted, peeled, and diced
- 1 large ripe tomato, diced
- 1 red or green bell pepper, sliced into strips
- 1 cup vegetable soybean, cooked
- ½ cup cilantro, roughly chopped
- ¼ cup pumpkin seeds

DIRECTIONS:

1. Spiral the summer squash through a spiralizer or use a vegetable peeler to slice it into thin ribbons.

2. Place the unsalted cashews, water, chipotle peppers, lime juice, and fine sea salt into a blender and purée until smooth, adding extra water if needed and scraping down the sides.

3. Pour the purée over the summer squash noodles and toss to coat. Divide onto 4 plates.

4. Top each plate of summer squash noodles with diced avocado, diced tomato, sliced bell pepper, cooked vegetable soybean, chopped cilantro, and pumpkin seeds.

Ingredient tip: You can steam the summer squash noodles for 1 minute if you want them to be slightly cooked but firm.

Per Serving: Calories: 252; Total Fat: 19g; Total Carbs: 16g; Net Carbs: 9g; Protein: 8g

SHERRY TOFU & SPINACH STIR-FRY

COOK TIME: 20 MIN | SERVES: 4

INGREDIENTS:

- 1 (14 oz) block firm tofu, pressed, and cubed
- 2 tbsp olive oil, divided
- Sea salt, fine
- 1 tbsp sesame oil, toasted
- 1 onion, thinly sliced
- 1 bunch spinach, stems removed and thinly sliced
- 1 tbsp garlic, minced
- 1 tsp ginger, grated
- ¼ tsp red pepper flakes
- ¼ cup low-salt soy sauce

- 2 tbsp sherry
- 1 (20 oz) can pineapple chunks, drained
- 2 scallions, finely sliced
- 2 tbsp sesame seeds, toasted

DIRECTIONS:

1. Heat the oven to 425°F gas mark 7. Cover a deep baking sheet with aluminum foil.

2. In a large mixing bowl, toss the tofu cubes with 1 tbsp of olive oil, being careful not to break them. Spread onto the baking sheet. Season with fine sea salt.

3. Place the baking sheet into the oven, and bake the tofu for 13 minutes, until gently browned.

4. Turn the tofu over and bake for 4 minutes to brown the other side.

5. In the meantime, add the remaining 1 tbsp olive oil and sesame oil into a heavy bottom pan over high heat until hot.

6. Add the sliced onion and fry for 4 minutes, until lightly brown.

7. Bring the heat down to medium and add the sliced spinach and cook for 2 to 3 minutes, until the leaves soften.

8. Mix in the minced garlic, grated ginger, and red pepper flakes, and cook for 1 minute.

9. In a small mixing bowl, whisk the low-salt soy sauce, sherry, and pineapple chunks.

10. Add the sliced scallions and soy sauce mixture to the pan and cook for 5 minutes, stirring frequently until the spinach is cooked and the flavor is incorporated.

11. Add the tofu to the vegetables and gently mix. Sprinkle with the toasted sesame seeds.

Per Serving: Calories: 244; Total Fat: 17g; Total Carbs: 9g; Net Carbs: 6g; Protein: 11g

SPICY CAULIFLOWER & HERB SAUCE

COOK TIME: 8 MIN | SERVES: 4

INGREDIENTS:

- ¼ cup cilantro, finely chopped
- ¼ cup parsley, chopped fine
- ¼ cup scallions, thinly sliced
- ¾ cup avocado oil, divided
- 1 medium lime, juiced
- 2 tbsp red wine vinegar
- 1 tsp cumin, ground
- Himalayan pink salt, fine
- Black pepper, ground
- 1 large cauliflower, cut into 4 thick slices
- 2 jalapeño peppers, thinly sliced
- 1 tbsp chili sauce or paste

DIRECTIONS:

1. Heat an outdoor barbeque grill or a cast-iron grill pan to high.

2. In a small mixing bowl, combine the chopped cilantro, chopped parsley, sliced scallions, ½ cup of avocado oil, lime juice, red wine vinegar, and ground cumin. Season the herb sauce with fine Himalayan pink salt and ground black pepper to taste and set aside.

3. Coat the sliced cauliflower "steaks" with the remaining ¼ cup of avocado oil and season with fine Himalayan pink salt and ground black pepper. Lightly char the cauliflower slices for 4 minutes on each side, until tender.

4. Place the cauliflower slices onto a serving platter and sprinkle with the sliced jalapeno peppers, and top with the herb sauce, and serve with chili sauce or paste on the side.

Substitution tip: you can swap the cauliflower for broccoli.

Per Serving: Calories: 242; Total Fat: 21g; Total Carbs: 13g; Protein: 5g

VEGAN THAI RED CURRY

COOK TIME: 5 MIN | SERVES: 4 – 6

INGREDIENTS:

- 2 medium English cucumbers, spiralized
- 1 cup enoki
- 1 cup basil, roughly chopped
- 1 cup mint, roughly chopped
- 1 tbsp olive oil
- 1 medium red and green bell pepper, cut into bite-size pieces
- 1 scallion bunch, sliced, and discard the ends
- 2 medium eggplants, sliced
- 1 (4 oz) jar Thai red curry paste
- ½ cup peanuts, chopped
- 1 lime, quartered
- Chili sauce or paste for serving

DIRECTIONS:

1. Place the spiraled cucumber noodles into a large deep bowl, and add the enoki, chopped basil, and chopped mint. Set aside.

2. In a large wok, add the olive oil and place over high heat. Add the chopped red and green bell peppers, sliced scallions, and sliced eggplants and cook for 5 minutes, stirring often for the ingredients to color and not burn.

3. Remove the wok from the heat and mix in the Thai red curry paste until all the vegetables are coated.

4. Spoon the hot vegetables onto the cold cucumber noodles and garnish with peanuts, lime quarters and have the chili sauce or paste on the side.

Substitution tip: you can swap the cucumber noodles for zucchini noodles or use spaghetti squash.

Per Serving: Calories: 313; Total Fat: 14g; Total Carbs: 22g; Protein: 13g

NUTTY ASPARAGUS ALFREDO

COOK TIME: 15 MIN | SERVES 6

INGREDIENTS:

- 1 cup cashews, raw and unsalted
- ½ cup deactivated yeast
- 1 large lemon, zested and juiced
- 2 tbsp garlic, chopped
- 1 vegan chicken, cubed
- 1 tsp Italian seasoning
- 1 cup water
- ¼ cup olive oil, plus 1 tbsp extra, divided
- 3 bunches asparagus, large and woody ends removed
- 1 tsp Himalayan pink salt, fine
- 1 tsp red pepper flakes

DIRECTIONS:

1. Combine the raw cashews, deactivated yeast, lemon zest and juice, chopped garlic, vegan chicken cubes, Italian seasoning, water, and ¼ cup of olive oil in a blender. Blend on high until smooth. Set aside.

2. To make the asparagus noodles, hold the asparagus tip and run a vegetable peeler down the length of the asparagus. Set the asparagus tips aside.

3. Place the asparagus noodles into a large colander set over a bowl, sprinkle with the fine Himalayan pink salt, and let it sit for 5 minutes.

4. Use your hands to wring the moisture out of the asparagus noodles, then return them to the colander.

5. Heat 1 tbsp of olive oil in a large heavy bottom pan over high heat. Fry the asparagus tips for 3 minutes and transfer them onto a plate.

6. Add the sauce into the same pan and warm over medium heat. Whisk for 10 minutes to keep it from clumping. Add the asparagus noodles to the pan and mix to coat.

7. Divide the asparagus noodle mixture onto 6 plates and top each serving with the fried asparagus tips and red pepper flakes.

Ingredient tip: deactivated yeast is also called nutritional yeast and referred to as nooch.

Per Serving: Calories: 302; Total Fat: 22g; Total Carbs: 18g; Protein: 13g

CAULIFLOWER AND LENTIL WRAPS

COOK TIME: 5 MIN | SERVES: 2

INGREDIENTS:

- 1 tsp avocado oil
- 4 cups cauliflower, riced or chopped
- 2 tsp chili powder
- 2 cups lentils, cooked or canned
- ½ cup pico de gallo
- 4 iceberg lettuce leaves
- 1 ripe avocado, pip removed and chopped
- 2 tbsp jalapeño pepper, sliced (optional)
- 2 tbsp low-fat coconut yogurt

DIRECTIONS:

1. In a medium heavy bottom pan, heat the avocado oil over medium-high heat. Fry the chopped cauliflower or rice and chili powder for 3 minutes until soft and fragrant.

2. Place the 4 lettuce leaves on a flat surface and evenly divide the cauliflower onto them. Top each with cooked or canned lentils, pico de gallo, chopped avocado, sliced jalapeño peppers (if using), and coconut yogurt.

3. Wrap one side of the lettuce leaf over the filling and fold in the sides and roll, repeat for the remaining lettuce.

Ingredient tip: pico de gallo is a salsa that contains tomatoes, onion, hot peppers, salt, lime, and cilantro.

Per Serving: Calories: 429; Total Fat: 19g; Total Carbs: 25g; Protein: 19g

LEGUME SWEETATO BALLS

COOK TIME: 20 MIN | SERVES: 4

INGREDIENTS:

- 2 tbsp olive oil, divided
- ½ onion, finely chopped
- 4 tsp garlic, minced
- 2 medium white sweet potatoes, peeled and grated
- 2 cups green lentils, cooked
- ½ cup almond flour
- 2 large eggs or egg replacer
- Pinch Himalayan pink salt, fine
- Pinch Black pepper, ground

DIRECTIONS:

1. In a large heavy bottom pan, heat 1 tsp of olive oil over medium-high heat. Fry the chopped onion and minced garlic for 3 minutes until soft. Add the grated sweet potatoes and fry for 2 minutes.

2. Remove the sweet potatoes from the heat and add them into a blender or food processor. Add the cooked lentils, almond flour, eggs or egg replacer, fine Himalayan pink salt, and ground black pepper and pulse until the mixture is well combined and holds together.

3. Roll the mixture into 32 balls.

4. In the same pan, heat the remaining olive oil over medium heat. Cook the sweet potato balls for 6 minutes on each side until browned.

Tip: this mixture will be great for homemade vegan burger patties.

Per Serving (8 meatballs): Calories: 331; Total Fat: 14g; Total Carbs: 37g; Protein: 16g

VEGETABLES & BEAN CURRY

COOK TIME: 20 MIN | SERVES: 4

INGREDIENTS:

- 1 tbsp canola or coconut oil
- 1 yellow onion, chopped
- 1 medium red bell pepper, seeded and chopped
- 2 tsp garlic, minced
- 2 tbsp curry powder or paste, mild or hot
- 1 (28 oz) diced tomatoes, canned and unsalted
- 1 (15 oz) can black beans, low sodium, drained and rinsed
- 1 large sweet potato, peeled and cut into chunks
- 1 cup coconut cream
- 1 cup kale, stems removed and chopped
- Sea salt, fine

DIRECTIONS:

1. Place a large heavy bottom pan, on medium-high heat and add the canola oil. Fry the chopped onion, chopped bell pepper, and minced garlic for 4 minutes until softened. Add the curry powder and fry for 1 minute until fragrant.

2. Add the canned tomatoes with their juices, rinsed black beans, sweet potato chunks, and coconut cream, and bring to a simmer for 15 minutes until the sweet potato is tender.

3. Remove the curry off the heat and stir in the chopped kale. Let it sit for 5 minutes until the kale has wilted. Season with fine sea salt to taste

Per Serving (2 cups): Calories: 275; Total Fat: 17g; Total Carbs: 29g; Protein: 8g

PROTEIN SPINACH CASSEROLE

COOK TIME: 15 MIN | SERVES: 4 – 6

INGREDIENTS:

- 1 lb. baby spinach
- 1 tbsp garlic, minced
- Sea salt, fine
- Black pepper, ground
- 4 large eggs
- 1 cup vegan parmesan, grated

DIRECTIONS:

1. Heat the oven to 350°F gas mark 4.

2. Fill a medium cooking pot with water and bring to a boil. Add the baby spinach into the boiling water and let it cook for 30 seconds. Drain the spinach and place it in cold water immediately. Drain again and squeeze out any remaining water.

3. Place the spinach into a medium mixing bowl and mix in the minced garlic, fine sea salt, and ground black pepper to taste. Place the spinach into a deep casserole dish.

4. Flatten the top and then make 4 shallow dips in the spinach. Crack an egg into each dip. Sprinkle the eggs with vegan parmesan cheese.

5. Bake for 10 minutes, until the egg whites have set

Per Serving: Calories: 200; Total Fat: 13g; Total Carbs: 5g; Protein: 17g

FRIED ALMOND PORTOBELLOS

COOK TIME: 8 MIN | SERVES: 4

INGREDIENTS:

- 4 large portobello mushrooms
- 2 large eggs
- 1 cup almond flour, heaping
- 1 tsp thyme, dried
- 1 tsp kosher salt, fine, plus extra to taste
- 1 tsp black pepper, ground, plus extra to taste
- 2 tbsp organic butter, unsalted
- 2 tbsp olive oil
- Celery leaves, for garnish
- 1 lemon, quartered

DIRECTIONS:

1. Remove the stems from the portobello mushrooms and place them to one side. Scrape away the gills and trim the edges of each cap to make it flatter.

2. Position 1 mushroom cap at a time in between two sheets of plastic wrap and flatten gently with the bottom of a pot or a meat tenderizer until it is about ¼-inch thick. Repeat with the remaining mushroom caps.

3. In a medium-sized mixing bowl, beat the eggs. In another medium-sized mixing bowl, combine the almond flour, dried thyme, fine kosher salt, and ground black pepper.

4. Dip each flattened mushroom in the egg, then into the almond flour mixture, repeat for a second coating. Do this for the remaining mushrooms.

5. In a large heavy bottom pan, melt the organic butter and olive oil together over medium-low heat.

6. Fry the mushrooms for 3 to 4 minutes on each side, until golden brown.

7. Sprinkle with celery leaves and add a squeeze of lemon on top and serve warm.

Per Serving: Calories: 269; Total Fat: 23g; Total Carbs: 7g; Protein: 10g

VEGETABLE LASAGNA

COOK TIME: 45 MIN | SERVES: 6

INGREDIENTS:

- 1 tbsp olive oil
- 1 (5 oz) packed baby spinach
- 2 tbsp garlic, crushed
- 1 cup basil leaves
- 1 large lemon, zested
- 1 (15 oz) ricotta cheese, low fat
- 1 large egg
- ½ tsp kosher salt, fine
- 3 medium zucchinis, thinly sliced
- 1 (25 oz) jar marinara sauce
- 1 cup mozzarella cheese, shredded or grated

DIRECTIONS:

1. Heat the oven to 350°F gas mark 4. Brush the bottom of a casserole dish with olive oil.

2. In a food processor add the baby spinach, crushed garlic, basil leaves, lemon zest, low-fat ricotta cheese, egg, and fine kosher salt and blend until smooth.

3. In the prepared casserole dish, layer the ingredients in the following order: zucchini slices, ricotta mixture, zucchini slices, marinara sauce, zucchini slices, ricotta mixture, zucchini slices, marinara sauce.

4. Bake for 30 minutes.

5. Sprinkle the mozzarella cheese over the lasagna and bake for 15 minutes.

6. Let the lasagna rest for 15 minutes before serving.

Per Serving: Calories: 283; Total Fat: 18g; Total Carbs: 17g; Protein: 17g

ITALIAN GOAT CHEESE FRITTATA

COOK TIME: 16 MIN | SERVES: 6 – 8

INGREDIENTS:

- 2 tbsp olive oil, divided
- ½ cup sun-dried tomatoes, diced
- 1 red bell pepper, seeded and diced
- 1 zucchini, chopped
- 3 tbsp garlic, minced
- ½ tsp kosher salt, fine
- ½ tsp red pepper flakes
- ¼ tsp Italian seasoning, dried
- 5 large eggs
- 1 tsp white wine vinegar, sweet
- 4 oz goat cheese, crumbled

DIRECTIONS:

1. Heat the oven to 375°F gas mark 5.

2. In a large nonstick cast iron pan, heat 1 tbsp of olive oil over high heat. Fry the diced sun-dried tomatoes, diced red bell pepper, chopped zucchini, minced garlic, fine kosher salt, red pepper flakes, and Italian seasoning for 5 minutes.

3. In a medium mixing bowl, beat the eggs and add the fried vegetables, sweet white wine vinegar, and crumbled goat cheese, mix to combine.

4. In the same pan, heat the remaining 1 tbsp of olive oil over high heat. Add the egg and vegetable mixture and cook undisturbed for 1 minute.

5. Place the cast iron pan into the oven and bake for 10 minutes, until the eggs are set.

6. Place the cooked frittata onto a plate and cut into wedges and serve warm.

Tip: adding 1 tsp of sour cream onto a frittata portion and sprinkled with chopped chives creates a different flavor to this dish.

Per Serving: Calories: 191; Total Fat: 14g; Total Carbs: 7g; Protein: 11g

ROOT VEGETABLE ROAST

COOK TIME: 30 MIN | SERVES: 4

INGREDIENTS:

- 1 lb. beets, peeled and quartered
- ½ lb. carrots, peeled and cut into chunks
- ½ lb. sweet potatoes, peeled and cut into chunks
- 1 tbsp olive oil
- 1 tsp apple cider vinegar
- Black pepper, ground
- Feta cheese, crumbled

DIRECTIONS:

1. Preheat the oven to 375°F gas mark 5. Line a baking tray with aluminum foil or non-stick cooking spray.

2. In a medium-large mixing bowl, add the quartered beets, carrot chunks, and sweet potato chunks, the oil, and apple cider vinegar and mix until well coated. Place the vegetables onto the baking tray.

3. Roast the vegetables for 30 minutes until tender and slightly caramelized.

4. Place the roasted vegetables into a serving bowl and sprinkle with crumbled feta cheese and season with ground black pepper. Serve warm.

Tip: sprinkle with fresh or dried mixed herbs for extra flavor.

Per Serving: Calories: 148; Total Fat: 4g; Total Carbs: 27g; Net Carbs: 15g; Protein: 3g

ZESTY MINT GREEN BEANS

COOK TIME: 5 – 10 MIN | SERVES: 4

INGREDIENTS:

- 1 lb. green beans, ends trimmed
- 1 tbsp avocado oil
- 1 medium lemon, juiced and zested
- 2 tbsp mint, finely chopped
- Sea salt, fine

DIRECTIONS:

1. Steam the trimmed green beans in a steamer pot with about 1 inch of water.

2. Bring the water to a gentle simmer and cover with a lid. Cook for 7 to 8 minutes over medium heat or until the green beans are tender.

3. Place the steamed green beans into a bowl and add the avocado oil, lemon zest and juice, and finely chopped mint leaves. Transfer into a serving bowl and season with fine sea salt. Serve warm.

Per Serving: Calories: 66; Total Fat: 4g; Total Carbs: 8g; Net Carbs: 4g; Protein: 2g

DESSERTS

NO-BAKE VEGAN CHEESECAKE BITES

COOK TIME: 3 MIN | SERVES: 4 – 6

INGREDIENTS:

- ½ cup almond flour
- ¼ cup almonds, sliced
- ¼ tsp kosher salt, fine
- 1 (8-oz) package cream cheese, vegan
- 3 tbsp sweetener, any of your choice
- 2 lemons, zested
- ⅛ tsp vanilla extract

DIRECTIONS:

1. Place the almond flour into a microwave-safe container and microwave for 1½ min to lightly toast it, set aside to cool. Repeat the same method with the sliced almonds.

2. Add the fine kosher salt into the cooled, toasted almond flour.

3. In a medium mixing bowl, add the vegan cream cheese, sweetener, lemon zest, and vanilla extract and mix until combined.

4. Spoon 1 tbsp of the cream cheese mixture and roll it in the almond flour to coat and set it on a plate. Repeat the same method with the remaining cream cheese mixture.

5. Place 3 or 4 toasted almond slices on top of each bite. Serve right away or place in the fridge for 1 hour and serve chilled.

Per Serving: Calories: 254; Total Fat: 22g; Total Carbs: 13g; Protein: 7g

LOW-CARB ALMOND CAKE

COOK TIME: 45 MIN | SERVES: 6

INGREDIENTS:

- 2/3 cup almond flour
- 1/3 cup applesauce, unsweetened
- 3 large eggs, separated
- 7 tbsp stevia sweetener, divided
- 3 tbsp organic butter, unsalted, melted, and divided
- 1 tsp vanilla extract or essence
- ¼ tsp almond extract
- ⅛ tsp sea salt, fine
- ½ cup almonds, sliced and toasted

DIRECTIONS:

1. Preheat the oven to 350°F gas mark 4.

2. Brush a 7-inch cake pan with 1 tbsp of melted organic butter and sprinkle 1 tbsp of stevia sweetener to form a thin coating on the bottom. Set aside

3. In a stand mixer fitted with a paddle attachment, mix the almond flour, unsweetened applesauce, egg yolks, 3 tbsp of stevia sweetener, 2 tbsp of melted organic butter, vanilla extract or essence, almond extract, and fine sea salt, until well combined.

4. In a medium bowl, using a hand mixer, beat the egg whites for 3 to 5 minutes, until soft peaks have formed, add and whisk in 3 tbsp of stevia sweetener.

5. Using a silicone spatula, gently fold the egg whites into the yolk mixture until well combined. Pour the batter into the prepared cake pan.

6. Bake for 45 minutes, or until the top is lightly browned and a toothpick inserted into the middle comes out clean.

7. Let the cake cool on a cooling rack.

8. In the meantime, scatter the sliced almonds onto a microwave-safe plate and microwave for 1½ minutes to toast. Sprinkle the toasted almonds on the cooled cake.

Tip: You can dust the cake with powdered sugar and add some fresh berries or make a berry compote.

Per Serving: Calories: 184; Protein: 7g; Total Carbs: 9g; Total Fat: 16g

DECADENT BLUEBERRY CAKE

COOK TIME: 20 MIN | SERVES: 8

INGREDIENTS:

- 2 cups almond flour, fine
- ½ cup Stevia or any granulated sweetener
- 3 tbsp coconut flour
- 1½ tsp baking powder
- ¼ tsp baking soda
- 2 large eggs
- 1/3 cup organic butter, softened
- 1/3 cup milk, low fat
- 1 tbsp vanilla extract
- 1 cup fresh blueberries
- 1 (8 oz) cream cheese block, cut into pieces
- ¼ cup almonds, slivered and toasted

DIRECTIONS:

1. Preheat the oven to 375°F gas mark 5. Line an 8-by-8-inch cake pan with parchment paper or use non-stick cooking spray.

2. In a stand mixer, combine the almond flour, Stevia, coconut flour, baking powder, and baking soda and mix until incorporated.

3. Add the eggs, organic butter, low-fat milk, and vanilla extract into the flour mixture and beat until well mixed.

4. Using a silicone spatula, fold in the blueberries and cream cheese pieces. Pour the mixture into the prepared cake pan, and top with the toasted almond slivers.

5. Bake for 20 min, or until completely set and beginning to brown around the edges.

Per Serving: Calories: 315; Protein: 8g; Net Carbs: 8g; Total Carbs: 12g; Total Fat: 27g

LIME & COCONUT TRUFFLES

PREP TIME: 25 MIN | MAKES: 16

INGREDIENTS:

- 8 oz cream cheese, softened
- 1 lime, juiced, and zested
- 6 to 7 drops liquid Stevia
- ¼ cup coconut, shredded and toasted
- ¼ cup macadamia nuts
- ¼ tsp sea salt, fine

DIRECTIONS:

1. In a medium mixing bowl, combine the softened cream cheese, lime juice and zest, and liquid Stevia and mix well. Cover with plastic wrap and place it into the freezer for 10 minutes to chill.
2. In a food processor, add the shredded coconut, macadamia nuts, and fine sea salt, and pulse until finely ground. Transfer into a shallow dish.
3. Spoon the cream cheese mixture out of the bowl using a 1 tbsp measuring spoon and roll into the coconut mixture to coat. Set in an airtight container. Repeat to make 16 truffles. Place into the fridge for 15 minutes before serving. Keep them stored in the fridge.

Tip: You can roll these truffles in toasted crushed almonds and coconut.

Per Serving: (2 TRUFFLES) Calories: 139; Net Carbs: 1g; Total Carbs: 2g; Protein: 3g; Total Fat: 14g

CHOCCHIP PB FRIDGE COOKIES

PREP TIME: 15 MIN | MAKES: 16

INGREDIENTS:

- ¼ cup coconut oil, melted
- ¼ cup plant-based butter, room temperature
- ½ cup peanut butter, natural salted
- ¼ cup dark chocolate chips, cut smaller if needed
- 6 to 7 drops liquid Stevia
- 2 tbsp sweetener, any brand

DIRECTIONS:

1. In a small mixing bowl, add the melted coconut oil, plant-based butter, peanut butter, chocolate chips, and liquid Stevia, and mix until well combined.

2. Place the peanut butter mixture into the fridge to firm up.

3. Use the 1-tbsp measuring spoon to scoop the dough out of the bowl. Roll it in the Stevia and place it into a container. Return the cookie balls to the fridge for 10 minutes to firm up. Placing these in the freezer will give you a firmer texture. The fat will keep them from turning rock hard.

Per Serving: Calories: 150; Protein: 4g; Net Carbs: 2g; Total Carbs: 4g; Total Fat: 15g

CHOCO MINT BITES

PREP TIME: 25 MIN | SERVES: 24

INGREDIENTS:

- 3 cups coconut, unsweetened shredded flakes
- ½ cup sugar-free maple syrup,
- ¼ tsp Stevia
- ¼ cup coconut oil, melted
- ½ tsp peppermint extract
- 6 oz 80% chocolate, chopped
- 1 tbsp vegetable shortening

DIRECTIONS:

1. Put the coconut flakes in a food processor and process until finely ground and nearly holding together.

2. Add the unsweetened maple syrup, Stevia, melted coconut oil, and peppermint extract, into a processor. Process until the mixture clumps together.

3. Form small cookies and place them on a baking sheet lined with parchment paper. Put cookies in the freezer and chill for 15 minutes or until firm.

4. In a heavy bottom pan, heat the chopped chocolate and vegetable shortening over low heat until melted, stirring occasionally.

5. Remove the pan from the heat and carefully dip each coconut cookie into the dark chocolate mixture, coating both sides.

6. Put the cookies back on the baking sheet and chill for 5 minutes in the freezer. Store in the fridge.

Ingredient tip: be extremely careful when you are working with melted chocolate. Do not allow any water or moisture to fall into it or else it will seize.

Per Serving (1 PEPPERMINT PATTY): Calories: 147; Net Carbs: 3g; Total Carbs: 6g; Protein: 1g; Total Fat: 14g

PB CHOCOLATE CUPS

COOK TIME: 5 MIN | SERVES: 12

INGREDIENTS:

- 1 cup coconut flour
- 1 cup organic peanut butter, chunky
- ½ cup Stevia sweetener
- 1 (9 oz) chocolate chips, Stevia-sweetened
- 4 to 6 tbsp creamer or plant-based milk

DIRECTIONS:

1. Line a 12-cup muffin pan with cupcake liners.
2. In a large-sized mixing bowl, add the coconut flour, chunky peanut butter, and Stevia sweetener and mix to combine. Divide the mixture into each prepared muffin cup and press it flat into the bottom of each lined cup.
3. In a bain-marie set over medium heat, melt the chocolate chips with 4 tbsp of creamer and mix well, add the remaining 2 tbsp of creamer if needed for a smoother texture.
4. Spoon the melted chocolate into each muffin cup.
5. Transfer into the fridge for 1 hour, serve chilled.

Ingredient tip: be extremely careful when you are working with melted chocolate. Do not allow any water or moisture to fall into it or else it will seize.

Direction tip: a bain-marie is when you have a pot of water simmering on the stove at the bottom and a slightly smaller one on top for the contents.

Per Serving: Calories: 320; Protein: 10g; Total Carbs: 27g; Total Fat: 21g

PISTACHIO & RICOTTA CHEESECAKE

COOK TIME: 1½ HOURS | SERVES: 8

INGREDIENTS:

- Non-stick cooking spray
- 1½ cups pistachio nuts, roasted
- 4 tbsp butter, unsalted
- 1 cup fat-free ricotta cheese
- 8 oz fat-free cream cheese
- ¾ cup sweetener, any of your choice
- 2 eggs, beaten
- 2 tsp vanilla extract
- 2 tbsp coconut flour
- 1 tsp sea salt, fine
- 1 medium lemon, juiced
- ½ cup cherries, pitted

DIRECTIONS:

1. Preheat the oven to 350°F gas mark 4. Coat a 9-inch springform pan with non-stick cooking spray.

2. Pulse the pistachios and butter in a food processor, until fine crumbs form.

3. Press the pistachio mixture into the bottom of the prepared pan and set it aside.

4. In a stand mixer, combine the fat-free ricotta, fat-free cream cheese, sweetener, beaten eggs, vanilla extract, coconut flour, and fine sea salt and mix well for 3 minutes, add the lemon juice.

5. Pour half of the filling on top of the crust in the springform pan, layer with pitted cherries and pour the remainder of the filling on top.

6. Bake for 1 hour.

7. Remove from the oven, set it on a cooling rack to cool to room temperature, and then refrigerate for a few hours or overnight before removing the cheesecake out of the springform pan and serving.

Tip: place a deep dish smaller than the inside of your oven, filled halfway with hot water. This will prevent your cheesecake from cracking in the center.

Per Serving: Calories: 347; Total Fat: 28g; Total Carbs: 14g; Protein: 12g

PB CHOCOLATE CUPS

COOK TIME: 5 MIN | SERVES: 12

INGREDIENTS:

- 1 cup coconut flour
- 1 cup organic peanut butter, chunky
- ½ cup Stevia sweetener
- 1 (9 oz) chocolate chips, Stevia-sweetened
- 4 to 6 tbsp creamer or plant-based milk

DIRECTIONS:

1. Line a 12-cup muffin pan with cupcake liners.

2. In a large-sized mixing bowl, add the coconut flour, chunky peanut butter, and Stevia sweetener and mix to combine. Divide the mixture into each prepared muffin cup and press it flat into the bottom of each lined cup.

3. In a bain-marie set over medium heat, melt the chocolate chips with 4 tbsp of creamer and mix well, add the remaining 2 tbsp of creamer if needed for a smoother texture.

4. Spoon the melted chocolate into each muffin cup.

5. Transfer into the fridge for 1 hour, serve chilled.

Ingredient tip: be extremely careful when you are working with melted chocolate. Do not allow any water or moisture to fall into it or else it will seize.

Direction tip: a bain-marie is when you have a pot of water simmering on the stove at the bottom and a slightly smaller one on top for the contents.

Per Serving: Calories: 320; Protein: 10g; Total Carbs: 27g; Total Fat: 21g

PISTACHIO & RICOTTA CHEESECAKE

COOK TIME: 1½ HOURS | SERVES: 8

INGREDIENTS:

- Non-stick cooking spray
- 1½ cups pistachio nuts, roasted
- 4 tbsp butter, unsalted
- 1 cup fat-free ricotta cheese
- 8 oz fat-free cream cheese
- ¾ cup sweetener, any of your choice
- 2 eggs, beaten
- 2 tsp vanilla extract
- 2 tbsp coconut flour
- 1 tsp sea salt, fine
- 1 medium lemon, juiced
- ½ cup cherries, pitted

DIRECTIONS:

1. Preheat the oven to 350°F gas mark 4. Coat a 9-inch springform pan with non-stick cooking spray.

2. Pulse the pistachios and butter in a food processor, until fine crumbs form.

3. Press the pistachio mixture into the bottom of the prepared pan and set it aside.

4. In a stand mixer, combine the fat-free ricotta, fat-free cream cheese, sweetener, beaten eggs, vanilla extract, coconut flour, and fine sea salt and mix well for 3 minutes, add the lemon juice.

5. Pour half of the filling on top of the crust in the springform pan, layer with pitted cherries and pour the remainder of the filling on top.

6. Bake for 1 hour.

7. Remove from the oven, set it on a cooling rack to cool to room temperature, and then refrigerate for a few hours or overnight before removing the cheesecake out of the springform pan and serving.

Tip: place a deep dish smaller than the inside of your oven, filled halfway with hot water. This will prevent your cheesecake from cracking in the center.

Per Serving: Calories: 347; Total Fat: 28g; Total Carbs: 14g; Protein: 12g

PEAR & CINNAMON BAKE

COOK TIME: 20 MIN | SERVES: 4

INGREDIENTS:

- 2 pears, halved lengthwise and cored
- ¼ cup almond flour
- 2 tbsp rolled oats
- 1 tsp maple syrup
- ½ tsp cinnamon, ground
- Pinch sea salt, fine

DIRECTIONS:

1. Preheat the oven to 350°F gas mark 4.

2. Place the pear halves, cut side up, in a square baking dish.

3. In a small mixing bowl, combine the almond flour, rolled oats, maple syrup, ground cinnamon, and fine sea salt and mix well. Add the filling into the pear halves.

4. Bake the pears for 20 minutes until tender and the filling is golden, serve warm.

Per Serving (1 pear half): Calories: 91; Total Fat: 3g; Protein: 2g; Total Carbs: 15g

CHOCO AVO PUDDING

PREP TIME: 5 MIN | SERVES: 4

INGREDIENTS:

- 3 ripe avocados, pitted and peeled
- ¾ cup almond or cashew milk, unsweetened
- 6 tbsp cocoa powder
- ¼ cup Stevia
- 2 tsp vanilla extract
- ¼ tsp sea salt, fine

DIRECTIONS:

1. In a blender, purée the peeled avocados, unsweetened almond or cashew milk, cocoa powder, Stevia, vanilla extract, and fine sea salt until smooth and creamy. Adjust the almond milk if needed according to the avocado size.

2. Place in the fridge to chill.

Per Serving: Calories: 282; Net Carbs: 4g; Total Fat: 22g; Protein: 5g; Total Carbs: 16g

MICROWAVE LEMON CAKE

COOK TIME: 2 MIN | SERVES: 4

INGREDIENTS:

- Nonstick cooking spray
- 1½ cups almond flour
- ¼ cup Splenda
- 2 tsp baking powder
- 1 tsp sea salt, fine
- ½ cup lemon, juiced and zested
- ¼ cup coconut oil, melted
- 4 large eggs

DIRECTIONS:

1. Spray 4 microwave-safe mugs with nonstick cooking spray.

2. In a mixing medium-sized bowl, mix the almond flour, Splenda, baking powder, and fine sea salt until combined. Add the lemon juice and zest, coconut oil and eggs, into the dry ingredients and mix until well combined.

3. Pour the batter equally into the 4 mugs. Microwave on high for 1½ minutes, or until cooked through.

Per Serving: Calories: 340; Total Fat: 30g; Protein: 11g; Total Carbs: 8g; Net Carbs: 5g

HEARTFUL PUMPKIN BITES

COOK TIME: 20 MIN | SERVES: 6

INGREDIENTS:

- 8 oz cream cheese, room temperature, and softened
- 1 egg, room temperature
- ¼ cup organic pumpkin purée
- ¼ cup Truvia brown sugar
- ½ tbsp pumpkin pie spice
- ¼ tsp sea salt, fine

DIRECTIONS:

1. Preheat the oven to 350°F gas mark 4. Prepare a 6-cup muffin tin with cupcake or silicone liners.

2. Cream together the softened cream cheese and egg in a mixing bowl, until smooth.

3. Add the organic pumpkin purée, brown sugar, pumpkin pie spice, and fine sea salt, mix until combined. Spoon the batter into the muffin cups.

4. Bake for 20 minutes, or until the center is slightly firm and not completely set.

5. Allow to cool for 30 minutes and place into the fridge until cold. Serve chilled.

Per Serving: Calories: 149; Total Fat: 14g; Protein: 4g; Total Carbs: 2g; Net Carbs: 2g

CHOCO CUPPA MOUSSE

COOK TIME: 5 MIN | SERVES: 8

INGREDIENTS:

- 4 oz 80% cacao dark chocolate
- 2 tbsp organic butter
- 3 eggs, separated
- 1 to 2 drops lemon juice
- ½ cup organic heavy cream
- 2 tbsp granulated sweetener of your choice
- ¼ tsp sea salt, fine
- 1 tsp vanilla extract

DIRECTIONS:

1. In a double boiler, heat the dark chocolate and butter over low heat for 3 minutes, until melted. Set aside to cool.

2. In a large-sized mixing bowl, use an electric mixer, and beat the egg whites with lemon juice until stiff peaks form.

3. In another large-sized mixing bowl, beat the organic heavy cream and sweetener until soft peaks form.

4. Mix in the egg yolks, fine sea salt, and vanilla extract into the cooled chocolate mixture, and fold in half of the whipped cream.

5. Fold the whipped egg whites into the chocolate mixture along with the remaining whipped cream, until mixed. Do not over mix or you will lose some of the volume.

6. Divide the mousse mixture into 8 serving cups and put them in the fridge to chill. To speed this up, put the mousse in the freezer and serve in about 10 minutes.

Tip: Beat the egg yolks till foamy then add them into the chocolate mixture and mix well to avoid scrambling. The heat from the chocolate will cook the eggs. If there are health concerns, use egg yolk powder and egg white powder and remove fresh eggs from the list.

Per Serving: Calories: 183; Total Carbs: 8g; Net Carbs: 6g; Protein: 3g; Total Fat: 15g

CONCLUSION

Congratulations for making the healthy choice to change your diet. Combining dietary changes with the medication your doctor has prescribed is a recipe for success. Receiving a type 2 diabetes diagnosis can knock the wind out of your sails. You have lost something important to you - your health.

It is not uncommon for you to go through the five stages of grief. You may deny it at first, looking for a second opinion or something else that may have caused your blood sugar to be high. And then you may have felt angry at yourself or your parents for giving you the genes that predispose you to the condition. Bargaining comes next. If you quit sugar for good maybe the diabetes will go away. When you realize that it is here to stay, depression might set in. But finally, you find yourself where you are today - accepting the diagnosis and planning the rest of your life.

Manufactured by Amazon.ca
Bolton, ON

22457135R00068